Four Women Doctors *of the* Church

Mary T. Malone returned home to Ireland in 1997 having taught for almost forty years in St Augustine's Seminary, Toronto, and in the University of St Jerome's, the Catholic College of the University of Waterloo. She is the author of several books, including *The Elephant in the Church: A Woman's Tract for Our Times* and the three-volume *Women and Christianity*.

Four Women Doctors
of the Church

Hildegard of Bingen
Catherine of Siena
Teresa of Ávila
Thérèse of Lisieux

—MARY T. MALONE—

ORBIS BOOKS

Maryknoll, New York 10545

ORBIS BOOKS
Maryknoll, New York 10545

Fathers and Brothers
MARYKNOLL™

Founded in 1970, Orbis Books endeavors to publish works that enlighten the mind, nourish the spirit, and challenge the conscience. The publishing arm of the Maryknoll Fathers and Brothers, Orbis seeks to explore the global dimensions of the Christian faith and mission, to invite dialogue with diverse cultures and religious traditions, and to serve the cause of reconciliation and peace. The books published reflect the views of their authors and do not represent the official position of the Maryknoll Society. To learn more about Maryknoll and Orbis Books, please visit our website at www.maryknollsociety.org.

Library of Congress Cataloging-in-Publication Data

Names: Malone, Mary T., author.
Title: Four women doctors of the church / Mary T. Malone.
Description: Maryknoll : Orbis Books, 2017. | Originally published: Dublin : Veritas, 2015. | Includes bibliographical references.
Identifiers: LCCN 2017002635 (print) | LCCN 2017019896 (ebook) | ISBN 9781608337057 (e-book) | ISBN 9781626982406 (pbk.)
Subjects: LCSH: Christian women saints. | Doctors of the church.
Classification: LCC BX4656 (ebook) | LCC BX4656 .M346 2017 (print) | DDC 282.092/52–dc23
LC record available at https://lccn.loc.gov/2017002635

Brigida claroptica Wexfordiana,
mulier fortissima et carissima

Contents

Introduction

There are now four women who are officially part of the *magisterium*, the official teaching body of the Roman Catholic Church. After two millennia of silence this is a revolutionary innovation, but it has passed the vast majority of Catholics by with barely a ripple of attention. These four women – Hildegard, Catherine, Teresa and Thérèse – have joined the ranks of about thirty male Doctors of the Church, including such giants as Augustine of Hippo, Bernard of Clairvaux and Thomas Aquinas. There is no sign in the documentation confirming the doctorates of these women that they are to be considered as mini-doctors, or doctoresses, but full and complete Doctors of the Church.

When the apostle Paul wrote in his first letter to the Corinthians around the year 55CE, 'Let the women be silent in the churches' (14:34-36), he inaugurated two millennia of diminishment of women's presence in Christianity. Nothing was required of women except silent and obedient presence. What they thought, how they theologised, and even how they prayed were considered to be entirely irrelevant. Instead, generation after generation of male teachers told women who they were, how they should think and act and even how they should pray. Women have been expected to live a kind of vicarious second-hand life, without any attention being paid to their specific needs and insights. As a result there was, for example, not one single Christian reflection for about two thousand years on the extraordinary but commonplace experience of conceiving a child, carrying a child, giving birth to a child and nourishing a child from one's own body. Instead, when male theologians looked at these experiences, they perceived something sinful and associated with original sin.

It was Pope Paul VI, in this as in so many other ways, who was the innovator here. Shortly after the Second Vatican Council, he requested the Pontifical Biblical Commission to look at the strictures of Paul against the teaching of women. They reported back that this particular word of Paul was indeed just that, a pastoral word of Paul, and not an expression of divine revelation. As a result, in the autumn of 1970, Pope Paul VI declared Catherine of Siena a Doctor of the Church, representing all laywomen, and Teresa of Ávila a Doctor of the Church, representing all religious women. This momentous event passed the Catholic Church by without a murmur.

It is obvious in the lives of these women that they are always conscious of their restricted role in the Church. Catherine complains about the limitations of being a woman. Teresa of Ávila is always conscious of the Spanish Inquisition constantly monitoring her audacity to teach as a woman. Even the mighty Hildegard comes up against ecclesiastical intransigence during her long life, leading eventually to the excommunication of herself and her whole monastery, shortly before her death.

So the teaching of these women is entirely significant to the Church today. This brief introduction is intended to awaken interest and open eyes to just one part of a magnificent but almost unknown tradition of the teaching of women Christians. A much more elaborate and analytical study is needed, but after two thousand years, it is time to make a start.

Mary T. Malone
Christmas 2014

− 1 −
Hildegard of Bingen

The life of Hildegard of Bingen offers us a vision of one of the most remarkable women in Christian history. As one of her monk secretaries remarked, she is, after the Blessed Virgin, the holiest woman who ever lived, and he was wont to address her, 'Hail, after Mary, full of grace'. He would probably be very surprised to learn that Hildegard was never canonised, though she has long been hailed as a saint in her native Germany, and in September 2012 she was established by Pope Benedict XVI as a Doctor of the Church. This chapter will examine the life, times and teaching of Hildegard, as we attempt to explore her greatness and blessedness, and some of the reasons why she was elevated to the same level as teachers such as St Thomas Aquinas and St Bernard of Clairvaux.

Hildegard lived at a time of enormous change in the Church, which we will explore briefly later. Here it is important to point out that she lived during the in-between time of two great theological movements that have had profound influence on the Church to this day: the ancient monastic contemplative tradition; and the dawn of the new and revolutionary development of Scholastic theology. She was not to live to see the flowering of Scholasticism, but she was aware of the first hints of this new theological stream. A Benedictine abbess for most of her long life, Hildegard was firmly rooted in the monastic tradition, which was more subjective and rooted in the experience of the monastic round of liturgical prayer than the more objective and systematic theology of Scholasticism.

Hildegard was born in 1098 to an aristocratic family in Bermersheim in southwest Germany. She was the tenth child and as such was dedicated to the Church as a tithe. Several other members of her family also entered the service of the Church. From the very beginning, she was marked as unusual and she herself tells us that from the age of three, she was aware of being in the 'shadow of the Living Light'. At the age of around eight, she was sent to the hermit, later Abbess Jutta of Sponheim, to begin a life wholly dedicated to the Church. The hermitage, which eventually became a full monastery, was situated near the Benedictine monastery of St Disibod, said to have been the Celtic monk who brought Christianity to the area. Here, she learned to sing the psalms in Latin, as well as understand some rudimentary aspects of the language. What makes her later writings difficult to comprehend is the fact that she never really mastered the language. In her mid-teens, Hildegard received the veil and made her profession as a Benedictine. For the next several years, the monastery grew in fame and numbers; when Jutta died in 1136, Hildegard was elected abbess at the age of thirty-eight.

Hildegard had feared the visions and voices that she had been receiving since childhood, and was afflicted with constant illness. In the year 1141, as she herself tells us very specifically, when she was forty-two years and seven months of age, she received her prophetic calling. She experienced a call to write down her visions and to use them for the reformation of the Church. From then on, for over thirty years, she was assisted by her secretary, the monk Volmar. He wrote down Hildegard's dictated teachings and corrected her Latin. For the rest of her life, Hildegard was a prolific writer. Her most important works in terms of religion are her trilogy covering the whole of Christian theology from the Creation to the end times. For ten years, from 1141 to 1151, she laboured at her best-known work, the beginning of the Trilogy, namely *Scivias*. This is an example of the way Hildegard used Latin as a personal form of expression. It stands for *Scito Vias Domini*, or *Know the Ways of the Lord*. *Liber Vitae Meritorum (The Book of Life's Merits)* occupied her from 1158 to 1163, and finally *Liber Divinorum Operum (The Book of Divine Works)* was completed in 1175, after twelve years of toil.

Even before *Scivias* was finished, word of Hildegard's wisdom and holiness had spread far and wide. The little monastery near St Disibod was overwhelmed with new applicants, so the abbess was forced to found a new monastery at St Rupertsberg, near Bingen on the Rhine in 1150, much against the opposition of the Abbot of St Disibod. Eventually, in 1165, she had to found a third monastery at Eibingen, across the Rhine, the only one that survives to this day. Word of her work was also reaching the ears of the highest and most esteemed members of the Church, Bernard of Clairvaux and Pope Eugenius III. In 1147, Hildegard wrote to Bernard of Clairvaux to ask his advice and look for a judgement on her writings, describing herself as 'wretched and more than wretched in the name of woman'. Twelfth-century society was very much aware, as was Hildegard, of the teaching of the apostle Paul that women were not allowed to teach, and there had been several public controversies about this. Bernard reassured her and to add weight to his reassurance, he brought *Scivias* to the Council of Trier, which Pope Eugenius was attending. The pope, a Cistercian, also reassured her and urged her to continue to do as she said, 'I write what I see'. Hildegard, he said, was obviously speaking for the Holy Spirit of God.

Hildegard's monastery at St Rupertsberg was like a village, with gardens, orchards, hospitality for the hordes of visitors and an infirmary for all who came for healing. It was here that the abbess engaged in several other activities. She was gifted with remarkable powers of observation, and she began cataloguing the illnesses, their diagnoses and their cures, as well as the qualities of all the herbs and medications. Hildegard, the scientist, is regarded as one of the founders of European pharmaceutical science. She produced two books, *Causae et Curae* and *Physica*, which was an encyclopedia of birds, beasts, stones, plants and remedies, to illustrate and explain her discoveries. We will return to all these works later.

From the early 1150s, Hildegard was engaged in a voluminous correspondence with popes, emperors, abbots, abbesses and people from all walks of life. Three hundred of these letters survive and make astonishing reading in their audacity and firmness. She had met Emperor Frederick Barbarossa around 1150 and alternatively sought his help and berated him for inflicting so much harm on the Church. The emperor was engaged in constant war with the popes, and in the course of his life appointed four antipopes to serve his interests. Antipopes were elected in opposition to the canonically chosen pope. From 1158, Abbess Hildegard set out on the first of four preaching journeys, which continued until she was in her late seventies. She travelled up and down the Rhine, and several other German rivers, preaching in monasteries, public squares, churches and cathedrals.

While all this intense activity was going on, Hildegard, as abbess, did not forget her nuns. She was intensely interested in liturgy and wrote many hymns, a musical drama about the virtues, *Ordo Virtutum*, and organised special liturgies for the monastery when she is said to have dressed her nuns in garments appropriate to the celebration. She took special care of the sick nuns and spoke to the male abbots about the necessity of new and different monastic habits for Benedictine women. Hildegard also cared for all the sick in the infirmary, washing them and applying herbal cures with her own hands. She never stopped writing and, among several other smaller works, she wrote a commentary on the *Rule of St Benedict.*

When Hildegard was eighty years of age, she was faced with the most serious crisis of her life when her convent was placed under interdict, or excommunication. This meant that for her and her nuns, there were to be no liturgies, no singing of the psalms and no more public work or writing of any kind. This all resulted from the arrival in the monastery of an excommunicated criminal, who, according to the abbess, confessed his sin and was reconciled to the Church before he died and was buried in the nuns' cemetery. When Hildegard was asked to exhume the body and produce it for burial outside the church, she refused. The interdict ensued and gave rise to a stream of letters to the local Archbishop of Mainz and to the pope. The nuns obeyed the interdict to the letter, but found their own ways to worship their God. Hildegard was especially outraged that the monastery singing had been forbidden, and prophesied dire punishment from God on those who had so decreed. Eventually, a few months before she died on 17 September 1179, the interdict was lifted. Public veneration of Hildegard began immediately, and even though several attempts were made to proffer her cause for canonisation, starting with Pope Gregory IX in 1233, all ended in failure. In the 1940s, all German dioceses were allowed to celebrate her feast. Later in the twentieth century, her music, drama and the illustrations of her visions became publicly known and greeted with astonishment.

It is time now to look at the context of Hildegard's life, so very different from our own, in a social and ecclesial sense. A twelfth-century context is essential to the understanding of her writings and her theology, as it is sometimes difficult for us not to interpret her as if she were our contemporary.

In the mid-twelfth century, a nearby abbess wrote to Hildegard criticising her for her habit of accepting only wealthy and aristocratic women into her community and not accepting poor women, as Jesus would certainly have wanted her to do. Hildegard's response is so revealing of her position as a member of the twelfth-century feudal aristocracy. She said that the divinely ordered and hierarchical universe, which was God's clear will, forbade her from accepting poor women. It would mean total disruption in her community. The poor women would become rebellious and the aristocratic women would be tempted to feel contempt for those beneath them. Above all, Hildegard wanted harmony in her monastery. Her abbess correspondent was obviously part of the new wave of those devoted to the evangelical life that was to be institutionalised by Francis of Assisi and Dominic Guzman in the Franciscans and Dominicans. It is equally clear that Hildegard's commitment still tended towards the old, now diminishing order of feudalism. In so many other ways, Hildegard mirrors the movements and temper of her times. It was an extraordinary century and the decisions made then have changed the nature and beliefs of Christianity down to our own day.

A list of Hildegard's contemporaries and the events through which she lived give us some small idea of the astonishing energy of her times. She gives us an example of how to live as a most devoted Christian in a most turbulent time. We have already met Bernard of Clairvaux, the founder of the Cistercians, and Emperor Frederick Barbarossa. Another extraordinary woman, wife of several kings of both France and England, spanned the twelfth century, like Hildegard. This was Eleanor of Aquitaine, whose father, interestingly enough, had died on pilgrimage to Compostela in repentance of his many and varied sins, which included the ownership of several episcopal sees and the appointment of their bishops. As part of the same feud between France and England and the papacy, Archbishop Thomas Becket had been martyred in 1170.

Other famous contemporaries included Héloïse and Abelard, whose star-crossed love story was as famous then as it remains today. Abelard stands at the dawn of a new age of theological scholarship. In his reading of the newly available writings of the early Church, he had found hundreds of disagreements on various points of Church doctrine. His book, *Sic et Non* (Yes and No), where he brings reason to bear in a new way on the solution to these difficulties, is one of the opening gambits of the scholastic age and the major work of Thomas Aquinas. It also prepares the way for the great universities, one of the glories of the age, many of which remain flourishing to this day.

In mid-century, Hildegard, together with Pope Eugene III and St Bernard, preached the Second Crusade. Islam had been the great external challenge to Christianity and with its spread, several of the most ancient Christian countries had been lost. At this period, Europe was on the offensive and Islam had been driven from both Spain and Italy. The First Crusade in 1095 had recovered some of the holy places and had established the Latin Kingdom of Jerusalem. This was now under threat and in 1144, a new Crusade was called. This was designed to arouse the Christian sentiments of the warring European countries, as well as to attack Islam. Eleanor of Aquitaine was one of those who tried to rouse the flagging spirits of Europe's fighting troops. This Second Crusade was to be a disastrous failure in itself and also in the centuries-long enmities and suspicions it aroused, of which we are only too well aware today.

The absolute focus of Hildegard's attention and commitment was what historians have called the

Gregorian Reform. This was an astonishing revolution in ecclesiastical self-perception, which has given the Church of our day many of its enduring facets, and has left us with some centuries-old unresolved problems. The reform is named after Pope Gregory VII, who, as a German priest, had accompanied one of the first reforming popes, Leo IX, to Rome in 1049. For the previous one hundred years the papacy had been disastrously exploited by several Italian families. It had been bought and sold and handed on as an inheritance by several popes whose only interest was to enrich their own families. Leo IX had brought this era to an end and had started the reform, which had been long awaited by many fervent Christians. In Hildegard's time, this reform was still trying to take root, as its tenets were so far-reaching that they would alter the experience of what it meant to be a Christian. The main object of the Gregorian Reform was to wrest the Church from the hands and influence of lay rulers and return it to the clergy. This meant that the Church would be totally in the control of the clergy, and it is from this element of the reform that the first universal law of imposed clerical celibacy was instituted at the Second Lateran Council in 1139. This law changed the face of Christianity definitively. Whereas chastity and celibacy had been strongly recommended to the clergy from the early days of the Church, it was almost universally ignored, so that by the early Middle Ages most clergy, including bishops and even popes – not to mention the lower clergy – were legitimately married, according to the norms of the time. Now all these marriages were deliberately revoked, causing huge social disruption as thousands of families were left destitute. Many were sold into slavery.

A deluge of propaganda against marriage, and women in particular, accompanied the Church's determination to make marriage an absolute impediment to priesthood. Marriage, and therefore women, was seen as the main obstacle to the relationship of the clergy with God and to their participation in the Gregorian Reform. It took centuries for this anti-marriage propaganda to work itself out in the Christian tradition. Gradually the expectation was created among all believers that priests should be celibate. When most clergy were married, they were completely integrated into the community. Now, the clergy became a separate caste in the Church and the understanding developed that, in fact, the clergy were the Church, and the Church was the clergy. It was this millennial-old understanding that the Second Vatican Council attempted to disrupt.

Hildegard of Bingen was a passionate supporter of the Gregorian Reform, still under way in her lifetime. She was devoted to the clergy and to the papacy, and was opposed to the four German antipopes of her lifetime, and to the notion of hierarchy as divinely ordained. In this hierarchy, there was no doubt whatsoever in her mind that those who lived chaste and celibate lives were, in this world, at the peak. All others, especially all the married, were much further down the ladder in God's design. In the anti-marriage propaganda, women and sexuality were practically equated, so it is no surprise that Hildegard was affected by these teachings and furthered herself from them.

As I mentioned earlier, it is very tempting to look at Hildegard of Bingen with a twenty-first century gaze, but she was a woman of her times in so many respects. In other ways, however, she radically outstripped her times with her multifaceted gifts and personality. It is time now to look at the teachings of Hildegard, both in the context of her times and, in a sense, *sub specie aeternitatis* (from a universal perspective).

The new interest in the *vita evangelica*, which was beginning to spread across Europe, was not the primary interest of Hildegard. This turn to the human life and activity of Jesus had been brought back to Europe by some of the surviving crusaders, who had been vastly moved by living in the places where Jesus had gone around 'doing good'. Translations of the Gospels into the newly developing vernacular languages of Europe helped spread this interest far and wide. The emphasis on chastity was now enlarged by a new understanding of the evangelical virtue of poverty, and new movements were gaining ground on all fronts, to be affirmed in the lives of Francis and Dominic and their communities in the next century. But Hildegard's primary interest was not here. She was a Benedictine in the ancient tradition of contemplation and there was a threefold focus to her whole life.

Hildegard was totally taken up by the utter incomprehensibility of God, whom she called the 'Living Light'. She tells us that from the earliest days of her childhood, she was conscious of this Light and that she felt herself to be living 'in the shadow of the Living Light'. This Light, Hildegard tells us, never left her and it is marvellously illustrated in her depiction of her visions. Her second focus was the all-embracing presence of the Trinity, again illustrated in the visions and in the multiple names she assigned to the Persons of the Trinity, as well as Father, Son and Holy Spirit. The third focus of Hildegard, who had been part of the ancient monastic tradition, is practically unknown to us, and that is her complete devotion to *Sapientia*, which is, perhaps, her favourite name for God. Hildegard was fully aware of the biblical tradition stemming from *Sophia*, a female embodiment of God, which had been allowed to lapse from consciousness with the emphasis on the all-male metaphorical Trinity. For those of us in the Church of today, this is perhaps the most radical part of Hildegard's teaching, but it occupies well near centre stage in her writings.

Before exploring further the teaching of Hildegard, especially in *Scivias*, her most systematic theological work, it is important to identify one of the most significant words and ideas in the whole corpus of Hildegard, and that is the word *viriditas,* which is usually translated as 'greenness'. Hildegard lived in the lush Rhine valley and writes with joy about the gardens and orchards of her monastery home. For her, the cycle of the seasons, especially the rising of the sap giving new life in springtime, was a primary metaphor of the spiritual life. *Viriditas* signified grace, the all-powerful presence of the Spirit and the all-pervasive presence of the Trinity. Hildegard saw aridity as a main sign of and metaphor for sin, and moistness and greenness as the principal sign of grace in our lives. We are told that she often concluded her letters with the words 'stay green and moist', which for her meant openness to the Spirit of God. It is an approach to life that takes us right into the twenty-first century, with its emphasis on the environment and on God's care for all of Creation. Hildegard's references to growing things, to clouds and rainfall and sunshine, to the shining of Creation, are abundant throughout her work. As she worked to tend the sick in the monastery infirmary, Hildegard was intensely curious about the properties and powers of plants, stones and herbs and wrote extensively on this. For her, this was all part of the greening power of God's Creation.

When Hildegard is writing about the actual workings of Creation and of the human body and its diseases, she is practical and scientific in her language. When she is writing of God and God's dealings with us in the mystery of salvation, however, her language changes completely; layer after layer of symbol and metaphor often leave the reader immersed in beautiful writing, but at a loss to reach the meaning. It is now time, however briefly, to look at Hildegard's theology and gain some understanding of the teaching of this amazing woman.

Scivias is a history of salvation told through visions in three sections, the first being on God the Father and the mystery of Creation, the Fall, the human race and the restoration of harmony after the Fall. Throughout, God the Father is the Living Light. The second section, again in visions, speaks of Christ and the work of salvation, leading to the founding of the Church. In her vision, Hildegard sees Christ as the 'man in sapphire blue', and the illustration shows this extraordinary blue human figure surrounded by the Living Light. It is here that she speaks of the importance of Baptism as our entry into this Light, and taking our place in the divinely created hierarchy of the Church, with its apostles, prophets, clergy, virgins and laity. It is interesting that during this period – with the emphasis on the clergy set apart through celibacy – the notion of the laity, also set apart, is entering theology for the first time. Hildegard is profoundly moved by the mystery of the Eucharist and she sees it as the wedding present of Jesus to the Church. The Liturgy of the Eucharist sums up the whole history of salvation and is our main weapon in our fight against evil. The third and longest section deals with the mystery of the Holy Spirit and our participation in this mystery. Hildegard speaks of the power of grace and outlines the virtues, all with female names, which are the basis of our participation in grace: *Patientia, Humilitas, Prudentia, Caritas*, and the greatest of all, *Sapientia*. The development of these virtues in our lives makes of us disciples who live with compassion, which is the surest sign of God's presence in our lives. The virtues act like the wall of the Temple, enclosing us in a sacred space, created by the mystery of the Incarnation, of the humanity of Jesus. Hildegard concludes with the end of time, when there will be great destruction and also great redemption, leading to ultimate harmony and eternal joy. Hildegard is a woman of great hope and optimism, but she is always conscious of what she calls the Antichrist, a symbol for all that militates against the Living Light. Despite her huge regard for the clergy, it is also they, the unworthy clerics, who are the objects of her greatest condemnation.

The whole of *Scivias* is illustrated by the visions of Hildegard. She tells us that her visions did not come to her in a state of trance, but that she was wide awake and saw them with the eyes of her mind, a kind of engagement in a process of symbolic thought. Her secretary, the monk Volmar, took her words, written on a wax tablet, and translated her convoluted Latin into readable prose. It was probably one of the nuns who did the paintings under Hildegard's direction. These paintings are astonishingly beautiful. During the Second World War they were brought to Cologne for safety and have not been seen since. Fortunately, the nuns at Bingen had made copies, so they are still available to us today. *Scivias* ends with the musical play, *Ordo Virtutum*, which, like all of Hildegard's music is a soaring tribute to the life of a disciple. In the prologue to *Scivias*, Hildegard writes:

> In the year 1141 of the Incarnation of Jesus Christ, the Word of God, when I was forty-two years and seven months old, a burning light coming from heaven poured into my mind. Like a flame which does not burn but rather enkindles, it inflamed my heart and my breast, just as the sun warms something with its rays. And I was able to understand books suddenly, the psaltery clearly, the evangelists and the volumes of the Old and New Testaments, but I did not have the interpretation of the words ...

Thus Hildegard describes the beginning of her writing career, under the command of God and the inspiration of the Holy Spirit. The resulting theological trilogy is, presumably, what constitutes the main reason why Hildegard was made a Doctor of the Church, as well as for her reforming zeal. Pope Benedict XVI cannot have been unaware of the content of her sapiential theology, centring on the naming of God as Lady Wisdom. While it is this section of her writing that is the most unfamiliar and most challenging to us, it was, in fact, a long-standing dimension of monastic theology, going back hundreds of years. Even though the naming of a female element in God results in either ridicule or horror today, it was part of the biblical naming of God that somehow got lost along the way. Hildegard probably marks the high point, and, in some ways, the closing chapter of this tradition.

Hildegard was the first woman to write reflectively about women in the plan of God. She did not challenge the traditional understanding of women as inferior to men, but she preceded the influence of Aristotle and Thomas Aquinas on western theology, and their teaching that woman was a *mas occasionatus*, an accidental man, or a mistake in creation. Hildegard's writing comes from the first millennium of Christianity. For her, as for Augustine, God intended to create both sexes from the very start. Men were created from the soil and therefore were strong and earthy; women were created from flesh and therefore were lighter, more frail and of a finer composition. It was God's explicit will, she thought, to call her as a prophet, frail woman though she was, to save the Church, since the clergy were being unfaithful to their calling. This theme of strength being perfected in weakness is central to her theology and is seen especially in her treatment of Mary as central to the mystery of the Incarnation. Hildegard's theology circles the three female characters of Ecclesia, Mary/Eve and Sapientia, Holy Wisdom, or the feminine element in God. Her visions give her the authority to preach and teach this theology to the whole Church.

For her, God is 'He who is' (Ex 3:14), to whom nothing can be added and from whom nothing can be taken away. God manifests himself to us in Trinitarian fashion through Love, Mercy and Goodness. The Creation was always there in the mind of God, as was each human being, and most especially Mary and the coming of Jesus. Hildegard's devotion to Mary is exalted and all-embracing because of her role in the Incarnation, but it may appear strange to us because of Hildegard's place and time. She lived before the doctrines of the Immaculate Conception and the Assumption, before the Pietà, and the image of the Mater Dolorosa, even before the Rosary. She also preceded the various apparitional titles. For Hildegard, Mary is the first representative of humanity, as Jesus is of divinity. Mary, as woman, represents the immanence of God, the presence of God in Creation and in each of us. Jesus, as male, represents the transcendence of God. The mission of humans is to continue to participate in Creation and in making God present to the world, as Mary did. The earth is our workshop of Creation. On earth and in marriage men and women are interdependent in love and in creativity, but the man is subject to God alone, while the woman remains subject to man.

The Incarnation is a perfect example of the conjunction of strength and weakness. Women know something of God's maternal love; men are not as familiar with this dimension. The male, however, can consciously choose his life, which should consist primarily of discerning good from evil. The female is assigned her place in life and does not have freedom of choice in the same way. Hildegard is here simply drawing theological conclusions from the normal social situation as understood by all at that time.

Nevertheless, it was Sapientia, Lady Wisdom, a female divine figure derived from the Book of Proverbs, that was central to her theology. As we have seen, Hildegard would have dominated any age, as she wrote her revolutionary new theology about the female face of the God of Wisdom, Sophia; as she composed her innovative new liturgies and liturgical music for her nuns; as she engaged in cutting-edge research on the pharmaceutical properties of herbs and other natural resources; as she publicly challenged popes and emperors, bishops and feudal lords; and, most of all, as she strode into cathedrals up and down the land preaching and teaching as God had directed her to do. We have no example of a woman of such presence and power in our Catholic Church today.

Nevertheless, what drove Hildegard in her time is available to us all today. It is the power of the Wisdom of God operating at the deepest level of our being. We need to be attentive and learn to pick up the cadences of this music in our lives. As a musician, many of

Hildegard's images are musical. She speaks of the soul as a symphony orchestra operating within us, with each musical instrument responding to God in its own way, but all in harmony. We have to be attentive to this 'inner reality', to the life going on within us. Hildegard was a Benedictine nun, and so despite her work and her travels, she had learned the art of attentiveness. It is the art we will meet again in the life of Thérèse of Lisieux, and in many other holy women. It is an art we can all learn in our own particular milieu.

— SUGGESTED READING —

Bruce Hozeski, trans., *Scivias* (Vermont: Bear and Company, 1986). This is the most popular and easily accessible of Hildegard's writings.

Matthew Fox, commentary, *Illuminations of Hildegard of Bingen* (Vermont: Bear and Company 1985). This book includes selections from *Scivias*, as well as some of Hidegard's other works, and reproductions of several of Hildegard's illustrations of her visions.

Barbara Newman, *Sister of Wisdom: St Hildegard's Theology of the Feminine* (California: University of California Press, 1987).

– 2 –

Catherine of Siena

atherine of Siena wrote her book *The Dialogue* at one of the worst possible moments in the history of the Church. Robert of Geneva, called the 'butcher of Cesena' because he was deemed to have organised the Church-sponsored murder of thousands of people in that city a short time before, had just been elected as Antipope Clement VII. The rightful pope, Urban VI, was in Rome but had been called the most hated pope in the history of the Church. Catherine herself had seen the destruction of some of her most fervent hopes for the reform of the Church. In a brief five days before leaving Siena for Rome, she dictated her book, with an amazing effusion of words, keeping three secretaries busy. It was October 1378. Catherine was thirty-one years of age and she knew that she was approaching the end of her life. No wonder her book was apocalyptic. It is the story of this heartbroken and heartbreaking woman that I am now going to explore.

Catherine Benincasa and her twin sister Giovanna were born, the twenty-fourth and twenty-fifth children of Mona Lappa and Giacomo Benincasa, a prosperous wool dyer of Siena on 25 March 1347, right in the middle of what has been called the 'calamitous fourteenth century' by the historian Barbara Tuchman. Catherine's twin sister died shortly afterwards and, in many ways, this haunted her throughout her life. Catherine grew up in a Church and world that were both in a state of devastation. The papacy had moved to Avignon at the beginning of the century at the behest of the French king in 1305. As we shall see later, this left Italy in a vacuum that was filled by warring states all vying for the power left by the absence of the papal court, with its cardinals and their huge retinues. Even more devastating, however, was the great tragedy of the fourteenth century, the Black Death, which, from 1348 on, devastated the whole of Europe, in particular Italy. It is believed that it killed between one- and two-thirds of the population of Europe. As far as most people were concerned, the devil was stalking the land, wreaking the vengeance of God on a sinful people. As many as half of Mona Lappa's children had died before the Black Death, but further tragedy haunted the Benincasas during the plague, as it did most of the other Sienese families. It is difficult to assess the effect of these double tragedies on an individual or a community, but it is fairly easy to understand the sense of the devil's presence, and the belief that a great war was taking place between God and the devil. The context of her birth also serves to explain some of the intensities that marked Catherine's life.

The consequences of the Black Death on the life of the Church are most noticeable in the following decades. Whole convents and monasteries had been wiped out, dioceses decimated and parishes left with a straggle of members. In an effort to replace lost religious and other clergy, little attention was paid to the quality of the candidates for vows or ordination, with the result that the Church was itself plagued with the most unsuitable ministers. As Catherine was later to write to Pope Gregory XI, the clergy were like 'demons incarnate' destroying the Church with their corruption. The cry for 'a few decent priests', which we shall also hear from Teresa of Ávila, was to haunt the Church for years afterwards.

Despite this we hear that Catherine's childhood was joyous and playful. There was a turning point at the age of six, when it is reported that while returning from her married sister Bonaventura's house with her brother, she saw a vision over the Dominican Church of Jesus wearing a papal tiara. This marked a total change in Catherine's life, and we are never again to see the joy and delight that seemed to have marked her early childhood. Catherine became quiet and stole away to pray. She even, at this early stage, began to avoid food and started to resist her mother's normal preparations for a daughter's marriage. Catherine was sent to her sister to learn the details of cosmetics and what we would call dating. This all came to an abrupt end when her sister Bonaventura died in childbirth. Henceforth Catherine's life was to take a path that marked out her journey to sainthood in the world of the fourteenth century. With an extraordinary sense of self-possession and independence, Catherine absolutely refused to marry, despite all her mother's machinations, and besides, she absolutely refused to become a nun. In retaliation she was appointed as the family maid, deprived of the privacy of her room, which she craved, and was coerced into serving the family as any other scullery maid would have done. Eventually, her father, who seemed to have had a much calmer disposition than Mona Lappa, having seen Catherine at prayer, decreed that all this should cease and that Catherine should be allowed to follow her own desires. The small room in which Catherine spent the following years is still on view in the Benincasa house in Siena today.

Catherine was in her mid-teens by now, and the exact circumstances of that period of her life, are, for the most part, unknown to us. We know that she spent the time in her room in total seclusion, that she deprived herself almost completely of sleep and food, and that her waking life was totally devoted to prayer. She tells us later about battling with demons and often crying out in despair to her God, but the foundations of her extraordinary life of prayer were laid at this time. We will explore her spirituality in more detail later, but, with such a context of tragedy, it is not surprising that her whole attention was focused on the Crucifixion, and on the love of the Trinity for us as demonstrated in the life and especially the death of Jesus. When Catherine later speaks about what we can learn from Jesus, she is usually thinking of his sufferings and his love for us. She rarely speaks of the parables of Jesus or other elements of Gospel teaching. Catherine did not speak, read or write Italian or Latin, but spoke only her own Tuscan dialect. It was only later that she learned to read and, towards the end of her life, to write.

At the age of about eighteen, Catherine expressed a wish to join the *Mantellate* – a kind of Third Order group of women who dedicated their lives to God in the Dominican tradition, but who took no vows and lived in their own homes. Most of the members were widows and initially there was great reluctance to admitting Catherine, but, as usual, she got what she wanted. These women wore the white Dominican habit with black cape, which signified purity and humility.

In 1368, at the age of about twenty-one, and after a mysterious experience of espousals to Jesus, who had by now become her most intimate friend and companion, Catherine tells us that she was instructed by Jesus to leave her solitude. From this time on, Catherine was rarely alone. Raymond of Capua, her confessor and intimate companion from 1374 to 1378, and her first biographer, tells us, probably quoting Catherine, that Jesus said to her, 'Leave me now; it is dinner time and your family are sitting down to table. Go and join them.' The ordinariness of this suggestion from Jesus gives us some idea of the calm intimacy that had developed between Catherine and Jesus. Raymond, who wrote her biography in 1395 when he had become Master General of the part of the Dominican Order that had remained faithful to Pope Urban VI, gives us many other intimate details about Catherine's solitary life. He tells us, for example, that she gave up wine completely at the age of fifteen, which illustrates at least one of the differences between the fourteenth and twenty-first centuries. In general, however, Raymond of Capua is writing hagiography and refers to Catherine as if she were already a canonised saint. He himself, although sixteen years older than Catherine, called her 'Mamma', as did all her companions, as we shall see. What we do get from Raymond, however, is a glimpse of how Catherine was seen in Siena by her contemporaries, once she had followed the instructions of Jesus and emerged from her solitude. She had spent the first twenty-one years of her life learning and being immersed in the love of God. Now was the time to go forth and live the other half of the Great Commandment, the love of neighbour. One final insight from Raymond for now is fundamental to Catherine's whole spiritual life. It is the teaching she had directly from God: 'I am He who is; you are she who is not. If you know these two things you will be saved.' This insight takes us immediately into the world of the earlier medieval mystics, such as Marguerite Porete, who had been the first (but not the last) woman mystic executed for her mysticism just thirty-seven years before Catherine was born.

This is not a psychological expression, telling Catherine that in the sight of God she was not worth anything. It is a deeper spiritual insight about the mystery of humanity and divinity. Later, God was to tell Catherine, 'I will make of you another me'. The whole spiritual mystical tradition rests on the principle that in the presence of God we are totally absorbed, and yet we remain our full selves. I will explore these insights more fully later when discussing Catherine's spirituality.

Catherine herself tells us that she hated the sight of human beings at the beginning of her journey into solitude. Now, starting with her family, her quickly growing group of friends, her community of Siena, the larger cities of Italy, and finally the whole Church was to receive the benefits of her loving attention and her total longing for the salvation of souls and the reform of the Church. This same year of 1368, when Catherine was twenty-one, her beloved father and supporter, Giacomo, died. He lived long enough to see the beginning of Catherine's public life, and was hugely criticised by the Sienese for his generosity in allowing Catherine to distribute much of the family's possessions as alms to the poor.

As Catherine began her work of serving the poor, the sick and the sorrowful of Siena, she was soon joined by a growing number of friends who were to remain faithful to her for the next ten or more years until her death. They included widowed relatives, such as her closest friend, Alessa; many clergy, Dominican and otherwise; several hermits who lived in a nearby forest;

other clergy who were university professors of scripture and theology; and several of the young nobles, men and women, from Siena. This little gathering came to be called her *famiglia,* and eventually, some or all of them accompanied her wherever she went. For someone who had relished total solitude, Catherine's eventual gift of friendship is astonishing. She had a horror of selfishness and saw in the sharing and communion of friendship a foretaste of heaven. Being friendless was, for Catherine, an experience of hell.

During these years of charitable work in Siena, Catherine's fame began to spread. Her gifts as a director and a reconciler drew thousands to her side, and we are told that a team of three priests had to accompany her everywhere in order to hear the confessions of those whose lives had been transformed by Catherine's life and teaching. Raymond comments in the biography that God had to send the Church 'mere women, fragile but chosen vessels' in order to show up the inadequacies of the clergy. The expression 'mere women' had often been used of women, and the implication of women's weakness confounding the strength of the supposed ministers of the Church is a frequent theme. However, as Catherine grew in confidence and in the understanding of her mission, she was anything but a mere woman. This young, uneducated woman in her twenties came to have the heart of a lion. She towered over the Church of Siena and often acted dictatorially and imperiously towards those whom she deemed not to be carrying out God's will. Even the popes were the recipients of her astonishing commands for the fulfilment of God's purposes. Where the reform of the Church was concerned, she would brook no opposition.

Much criticism was directed at Catherine for several reasons. One was the obvious reason that she was engaging in all this activity as a woman, when she should have remained in her cell, as the other members of the *Mantellate* did. Catherine's response was to direct people's attention to the cell of the heart. Again, this became one of the central elements of her spirituality. We must each develop an inner cell of self-knowledge, to which we can retire, and where we can meet God face to face. Much criticism was directed at the motley group of friends who always surrounded her: clergy, religious, married and unmarried women, and men. Siena had never seen anything like it; all the traditional demands for the seclusion of married women and the total separation of women and men seemed to be totally ignored by Catherine and her *famiglia*. But the greatest criticism of all was directed at Catherine herself and her extraordinary inability to eat. Raymond of Capua tells us that she ate hardly anything and survived on about one hour's sleep every few days. This *inedia* or inability to eat, which was so characteristic of Catherine's life, is a bit of a mystery. Whether she totally destroyed her digestive system in her years of solitude, or whether, as some suggest, it was a psychological reaction to the death of her twin and so many others during the years of the successive plagues, the real reason remains hidden. Catherine herself tells us that she tried to eat at least some raw vegetables and bread once or twice a day, but food made her intolerably ill. Because of her public ecstasies during Communion when she attended the public liturgy, her directors cut down her opportunities for Communion. Eventually, when Raymond of Capua was appointed her director by the Dominican Order, he restored this privilege to her and told her to receive Communion as often as she wished. From then on, from 1374 until her death in 1380, Catherine seems to have survived on the Eucharist alone.

The year 1374 was a momentous year in Catherine's life. Raymond of Capua became her friend and director, and she began her travels outside Siena. The first of these was to Florence. To put this trip in context, we must return to 1370. On 30 December that year, Pope Gregory XI was elected pope in Avignon. His predecessor, Urban V, had returned to Rome from 1367 to 1370, but then chose to go back to Avignon. He never made it, but died at Anagni. It was this personal choice of the pope to return to Avignon that shocked the faithful of Europe, as it was under coercion from French kings that other popes had gone and remained there. As most of the Avignon popes were French, a longing began to be expressed in Italy for their own pope, a Roman.

With the election of Pope Gregory XI, Catherine set all her energies towards three aims. The first was to get the papacy back to Rome with an Italian, and preferably a Roman pope. Secondly, she wholeheartedly supported one of the first actions of Pope Gregory, namely the calling of a crusade. In Catherine's mind, the crusade was not primarily concerned with the defeat of the infidels in far away Jerusalem, though this aim was certainly there. Much more so, she saw it as arousing the Christian spirit of the people, and stopping the endless warfare that was tearing Europe, and more immediately, Italy, apart. The Tuscan League was a group of Italian cities, led by Florence, which was organised against the pope, his interests, his armies and his wealthy cardinals and retinue. It was in the context of these fratricidal wars that Cardinal Robert of Geneva, leading the papal troops, had been engaged in the massacre of Cesena. For Catherine, the crusade would solve all the Church's problems, as well as removing all the fighting forces from Europe. Her third goal was the reform of the Church, which for her meant the restoration of a devout and holy priesthood who would restore dignity and sanctity to the celebration of the Eucharist and the administration of the sacraments. Then, without a doubt, the laity would follow.

The energy expended by Catherine on these three goals was astonishing. It started with a letter-writing campaign that included many of the crowned heads of

Europe, as well as cardinals, bishops, abbots and the nobility of Siena and the Italian cities. We have about four hundred of her letters, many of them directed specifically to the crusade. It absorbed all her attention and made her a devoted follower of Pope Gregory XI, whom in her letters she called 'my sweet Babbo' and 'sweet Christ on earth'.

The immediate reason for her journey to Florence, her first journey outside Siena, was a summons by the Dominican general chapter meeting in that city. We do not know the exact reason for this but we do know that Dominican opinion was much divided about this female associate of theirs who was garnering more attention than all the rest of the Dominicans put together. Her detractors called her hare-brained and a hypocrite because of her apparent inability to eat. They suggested that in private she feasted gaily with her friends. However, the outcome was one of the great gifts of her life. She was given Raymond of Capua as her confessor, and for the next four years, from 1374 to 1378, they were practically inseparable. Catherine wrote some of the most beautiful words on friendship as a result of this relationship. She said that God commands us to love all, but that sometimes we are sent a most particular friend whom we love freely and without bounds. This love, she says, is not as the result of a command but of two hearts veering inexorably towards each other. 'The love with which I love myself, that is the love with which I love my friend.' 'This is how it is with very dear friends,' she says. 'Their loving affection makes them two bodies with one soul, because love transforms us into what we love.' And speaking to her wider *famiglia*, she says, 'Don't let cowardice keep you from loving.' Raymond became a member of the *famiglia*, and like all the others, called her 'mamma'. It is astonishing that this young woman, who spent most of her early life totally secluded from the world, could discover and live the deep meaning of friendship. She speaks of 'devouring the faces of her friends', and all who met her were surprised at the intensity with which she presented her whole attention and love to each.

While in Florence, the same explosion of conversions followed Catherine, and the Dominicans appointed three of their number to follow her everywhere from then on to deal with the conversions. Raymond agreed with Catherine on the forthcoming crusade, and together they preached, cajoled and encouraged the fighting men of Europe and their leaders to adopt this noble cause. Catherine returned from Florence to Siena in June 1374 and found another outbreak of plague ravaging the city. All thoughts of crusade were set aside as she tended the sick and dying. There was no cure for the plague, so the only remedy was to help people to die well, and they did in their thousands. Catherine herself lost several members of her family, in particular nieces and nephews, to the horror. One-third of the population of Siena died and all public life was at a standstill. Dozens of women were widowed and the ranks of the *Mantellate* grew, this time including Catherine's sister-in-law, Lisa, who became one of her closest friends, and Catherine's mother Mona Lappa, who was now one of her daughter's most devoted followers and outlived her by decades.

In 1375, the Dominicans in Pisa invited Catherine to initiate a reform of the Church community there. Catherine was thrilled because it gave her an opportunity to preach the crusade and to plead with the people of Pisa and Lucca not to join the Tuscan League against the pope. Here her pleadings failed as both cities, as well as Siena, eventually joined the League. There was the usual stream of conversions in Pisa, but for Catherine two great additions to her deepening spirituality took place. She tells us, and this is confirmed by Raymond, that she received invisible stigmata, which united her even more to the crucified Jesus who was the centre of her life. But on a more human level, Catherine saw the sea for the first time and was totally entranced by its mystery, depth, richness and immensity. From now on a flood of sea metaphors appear in her writings, and this links her to so many of the earlier medieval mystics.

By the end of 1375, all of Italy was in arms against the Church and all thoughts of a crusade were terminated. Pope Gregory XI put the city of Florence under interdict and the whole city came to a standstill. Catherine felt the enormous burden of the Church on her shoulders. She offered to go to Avignon to plead Florence's cause with the pope, and write to the pope to awaken him to the devastation of the Church in Italy. This was Catherine at her most dictatorial, a woman of twenty-nine ordering the pope to 'do what you have to do manfully and with the fear of God'. Earlier in the letter she berates the pope for not choosing the right cardinals. 'I have heard that you have created cardinals. I believe that it would be more to the honour of God and better for yourself if you would always take care to choose virtuous men.' Early in 1376, Pope Gregory promised Catherine that he would return to Rome before the end of the year. It seemed that at least one of her hopes would be fulfilled.

In mid-year, Catherine eventually set out for Avignon at the request of Florence. She left with over twenty members of her *famiglia* via Bologna and Marseilles. Two days after arriving in Avignon, Catherine met Pope Gregory XI for the first time. Catherine was astonished and shocked at the papal court. The life there was a revelation to her with the multitude of womenfolk surrounding the cardinals and the basic lack of any kind of religious fervour. The women ridiculed her, stuck pins in her feet as she prayed and even the Florentine ambassadors disowned her, even though it was on their behalf that she had come. However, Catherine, with her single-minded intention of getting the pope back to Rome, pursued her own unwavering course. She and the pope could not actually communicate directly since Catherine only spoke the Tuscan dialect, but her faithful friend Raymond did the translations.

In September 1376, to Catherine's great delight, Pope Gregory XI finally left Avignon for Rome, after practising what Catherine called a 'holy deceit' in leaving quite suddenly and unexpectedly. Catherine left Avignon for Siena the same day, accompanied by a portable altar for daily Mass, with the pope's permission, and her three confessors as well as Raymond and her friends. They arrived in Siena just before Christmas, and eventually, in January 1377, Pope Gregory XI sailed up the Tiber and established the papacy once more in Rome.

The year 1377 was a busy one for Catherine. She had been given a property at Belcaro outside Siena by a nobleman and had received permission from the pope to establish a convent there. She eventually moved there with her retinue. This was also the year of the massacre at Cesena and Catherine was shocked that despite her urging, Pope Gregory did not condemn it. She spent a good part of the year mediating a family feud with one of Siena's most noble families, which brought her a lot of criticism, the details of which need not detain us. Florence, Siena and the other Italian cities were still at war with the pope and used the tragedy of Cesena against him. Catherine was shocked at the pope's lack of reforming initiatives and she wrote to him that he should resign if he was not going to reform the Church. This letter shocked the pope and for a time created a rift between them. Catherine was unfazed and advised the pope to 'mitigate your anger with the light of reason and with truth. ... To whom shall I turn if you abandon me? ... I will hide myself in the wounds of Christ crucified, whose vicar you are.' Eventually, peace was restored between them and the pope asked Catherine to go to Florence to try to broker peace in early 1378. A Peace Conference was just about to take place when Pope Gregory died on 27 March 1378. Two days before, Catherine had celebrated her thirty-first birthday. Again, Catherine's dreams were dashed, but as she herself prophesied, much worse was to follow. On 8 April the new pope, Urban VI, a Neapolitan, was elected. The conclave had been somewhat of a farce in ways, but Pope Urban had led a fairly unblemished life and the Romans accepted him. The problem was that Pope Urban was a rabid reformer. It was not long before his harsh attitudes revealed themselves. The cardinals cowered before his rages and rudeness. Catherine, on hearing this, wrote to the pope in her typically direct and inflexible way: 'justice without mercy is clouded with cruelty.' She urged him to create some new and stalwart cardinals, but that did not happen. As the summer heat approached, the French cardinals who were in the majority withdrew gradually from Rome, and Catherine realised that the signs were ominous. Most of the curia followed and the French cardinals assembled an army. Sure enough, on 9 August, the French cardinals declared the Papal See vacant and proceeded to elect a new pope. Three of the cardinals were Italian, and Catherine wrote them a bitter letter, fuming with anger, accusing them of betrayal, infidelity and of being 'ungrateful, coarse and mercenary'.

On 20 September 1378, the cardinals elected a new pope, an antipope, a man whom we have met before. He was Cardinal Robert of Geneva, the 'butcher of Cesena', who took the name Clement VII. Catherine wrote to Urban in profound distress. 'Alas, alas, alas, my sweet Father, with pain and sorrow and great bitterness and tears I write this ... I find around you, Christ on earth, a hell of iniquity, and the poison of self-love.' She promised to remain faithful to him 'for the glory and praise of the name of God and for the reforming of Holy Church'.

Urban sent for her to come to Rome and Catherine prepared to leave Siena knowing she would not return. Raymond of Capua had earlier been appointed Prior of the Church of the Minerva in Rome, and she was more than happy to be united with him again. In early October, as previously mentioned, Catherine dictated her book, *The Dialogue*, in a marathon of energy. Words poured out of her and kept three secretaries busy. On hearing of the election of the antipope, she had written to Urban, 'I have heard that those demons in human form have elected an anti-Christ against you. Now forward, most Holy Father! Go into this battle without fear.'

We shall examine her book later, but for an entirely unplanned work it is quite remarkable. It covers the whole mystery of salvation, with Jesus – the Bridge – at the centre of God's plan. It is definitely not an easy read, with repetitions and a layering of ideas that can be dizzying. But it is possible to follow the thread of her argument and pick out the main mystical themes that had governed her life.

At the end of November, Catherine arrived in Rome with some of her retinue. No sooner had she arrived than she heard that Pope Urban had sent Raymond on a mission to the King of France. She was again devastated, and the description of her desolation, kneeling on the banks of the Tiber as Raymond departed, is indeed heartbreaking. They would never meet again, even though they continued to communicate by letter. Catherine found Rome to be a battlefield as the armies of the antipope attacked and defended Castel Gandolfo and blocked Urban's access to the sea. During the month of December, Catherine saw Urban frequently and he used her presence and gifts as a political tool. He excommunicated the antipope and all his followers. He created new cardinals and then tortured them to see if they harboured any secrets against him. Catherine was one of the few voices of reason in this desperate situation. Mona Lappa and other friends arrived for Christmas, but celebration was the furthest thing from anyone's mind.

This situation continued with little change throughout 1379. Catherine's health was deteriorating and each day she dragged herself about a mile to St Peter's for Mass and remained in prayer till vespers. Eventually she suffered what seems to have been a stroke, and was given permission to have Mass in her house when she could no longer even move from her room. But there was little joy for Catherine. Much of the Church now turned against her because she had initiated the return of the pope from Avignon. If she had not interfered, things would be so much better. Even some of her closest friends turned against her. One of her final acts was to dictate a letter to Raymond telling him to take charge of all her writings and to look after her friends.

As a result of the schism, the whole Church was in turmoil. All countries, dioceses, parishes, monasteries and convents were split in two and their members took sides with either Urban or Clement. Even the Dominicans split and, shortly after her death, when Raymond of Capua was elected Master General of the Dominicans, he was in charge of only half an order. The other half had followed his predecessor, Fr Elias, to side with the antipope. Reform was even further away, and for almost one hundred years this state of affairs continued with pope and antipope continuing to be elected. Looking back from the twenty-first century, one cannot help reflecting that it is a miracle the Church has survived.

Catherine died on 29 April 1380, in the arms of her most faithful friend, Alessa. She was buried in the Church of the Minerva in Rome where her body still rests. As was the custom then, her head was later removed and carried in a huge procession to the Dominican church in Siena by Raymond of Capua in April 1384. Among those in the procession were Catherine's *famiglia*, led by old Mona Lappa, her mother. Raymond finished Catherine's biography in 1395 and he died in 1399.

In 1461, Pius II, a Sienese pope, issued the Bull of her canonisation. Her feast is celebrated by the Universal Church on 30 April, but in her home in Siena it is celebrated the previous day, the day of her death. In October 1970, Pope Paul VI declared her a Doctor of the Church, representing all laywomen. On the same day, Teresa of Ávila, representing all religious women, was also declared a Doctor of the Church.

It is time now to look at Catherine's spirituality and her teaching, as shown in her writings. We have her *Dialogue*, almost four hundred letters, and a collection of prayers, mostly written during her final days in Rome. Catherine was not a systematic writer, but the same themes keep emerging all through her writing. Catherine's *Dialogue* is recognised as one of the great late medieval mystical texts. It differs enormously from the mystical writing of her great English contemporary, Julian of Norwich (1342–1416). It is most unlikely that they ever heard of each other, and no two women could have led such dissimilar lives at that time. Julian's life in her cell was calm and serene and she seemed to be quite unaware of the ecclesiastical chaos happening around her. Catherine's life, after her early period of solitude, was a headlong rush to reform the Church. She involved herself in every crisis and, so to speak, did her mysticism on the run. Catherine's mysticism was her whole life and was integrated into every moment, every project and every piece of her writing.

What is mysticism? Quite simply, it is the experience of direct access to God, not a theory, but an actual experience. Even though Catherine seemed to be quite unaware of the great women mystics who preceded her throughout the Middle Ages, like Mechthild of Magdeburg, Gertrude the Great and Marguerite Porete, the same themes and quality of prayer link her to them. Women's mysticism differs distinctively from that of men in its origins and aims. Whereas men seek to shatter their worldly personae and conform their lives to the will of God, and therefore, for the most part, have to retire into solitude away from the world, women, basing themselves on the *imago dei* (image of God), seek intimacy and even identity with God and then seek to enter the world to engage in the public exercise of compassion. In much of the writing about male mysticism, it is described as a most precious gift available only to the few; women mystics, on the other hand, always insist that mysticism is for everyone, and offered to all without exception.

For several reasons, Catherine's mysticism was a blend of the two. She speaks constantly about acting manfully to reform the Church, since the men have failed to do so, and she urges pope and priest to do the same. On the other hand she says that the greatest sin we can commit is not to recognise God in ourselves, and tells us that God had told her 'I will make of you another me' in an act of intimacy and identity. Catherine's spirituality and faith is dualistic, most understandably because of the horror of the times. She sees life as a constant war between flesh and spirit, hell and heaven, the devil and God. She is constantly warring with the devil who, she tells us, calls her a 'damnable woman' because he can make no headway with her. The devil is a very deep reality for her, as is hell and eternal damnation. She sees the devil as God's minister of justice assigning due punishments to the unrepentant. Thus repentance plays a major role in her life and in her teaching to others. For this reason, she has enormous devotion to 'dear Magdalene' whom she mentions constantly as one of her guides and inspirations. It is interesting that Julian of Norwich, hidden in her peaceful cell, did not believe in hell because of her enormous faith in the love of God. Her famous words, 'All will be well and all will be well and all manner of thing will be well' would probably have sounded rather too optimistic to Catherine, despite her enormous trust in the Providence of God. Catherine's actual experience was of everything in the Church not going well, in fact going from bad to worse.

The first words of *The Dialogue* marvellously sum up the whole of Catherine's life.

A soul rises up restless with tremendous desire for God's honour and the salvation of souls. She has become accustomed to dwelling in the cell of self-knowledge in order to know better God's goodness towards her since upon knowledge follows love. And loving, she seeks to pursue truth and clothe herself in it.

Catherine further tells us that the 'home of self-knowledge was opened for us at Pentecost, when the Holy Spirit took up residence among us'. Truth was one of her primary goals, and one of her favourite names for God was 'First Truth'. The word 'restless' is one of the important words in that first sentence. Catherine simply could not rest when work for God needed to be done. 'I have only this small moment in time,' she said, and God also told her, 'I make you free so that you are subject to no other except me.' This is the hallmark of the woman mystic, and one of the reasons why Catherine rarely delayed in asking permission or direction, but rushed ahead to defend God's honour, as she believed she was being led to do. As she, a young uneducated woman, tried to rouse the Church to the needed reforms, she said one day to Jesus, 'My very sex, as I need not tell you, puts many obstacles in the way. The world has no way for a woman to mix so freely in the company of men.' And Jesus replied to her, 'With me there is no male or female.' This shows that Catherine was very much aware of the criticisms directed at her by both Church and society, but criticism never stopped her restless rush forward. She had, as she herself said, and urged others to do also, 'come to grips with the image of God in herself'.

Again, although apparently quite unknown to Catherine, many of her new sea metaphors picked up on the themes of previous mystics. She wrote: 'The more I enter, the more I discover, and the more I discover, the more I seek.' This is so reminiscent of the marvellous words of Hadewijch of Brabant, who was also enamoured by the sea as an image of God's attraction and immensity. 'I swim towards the shore, only to find that you have enlarged the sea. Then you strengthen my desire and give me more muscle to swim again towards you.' Or again, it is a reminder of the words of Marguerite Porete, who described the Seine entering the sea, and then not knowing where the river ended and the sea began, or where humanity ended and divinity began.

Catherine's favourite and central image of Christ in *The Dialogue* is of Christ the Bridge. Many suggest that she was thinking of the bridge over the River Arno in Florence. Christ is the bridge between humanity and divinity and we can cross freely and without payment on this bridge. Believers and those who love and do justice to the poor cross safely, but those who steal from the poor, whether clergy or lay, fall off the bridge and are lost in the mire. Catherine even suggests that some fathers throw their daughters off the bridge in order to make money and the women are never recovered.

As part of this image, Catherine describes the three traditional stages of spirituality, though she uses imagery and not theory. She is describing the stages of purgation, illumination and union, as all the previous generations of Christians understood them. Purgation represented the initial stage where we prepare ourselves to begin the journey by getting rid of all the unnecessary baggage that separates us from God. Then the mind and heart are illuminated – and most mystics use this word – and the things of God seem to enter the spirit easily and joyfully. We are given the gift of discernment and learn how to choose the good and avoid the ancient tempter, as Catherine would say. Finally we are given the gift of union where humanity and divinity seem to merge into one being and, though briefly, we become one with God. As Catherine heard so often from her Creator, 'I will make of you another me'.

For Catherine, these stages are represented by the feet, heart and mouth of the crucified Jesus. The feet teach us to walk in the right direction or, as Catherine says in another of her sea metaphors 'sail with the right wind'. At first we may walk the way of God for fear of punishment, but eventually we will learn true humility, which is a deep realisation of our gifts and of the gift of

God's image imprinted on our being. Then we can enter the heart of Jesus where the way of love will be revealed to us. And, as always for Catherine, love and knowledge are deeply intertwined. Love illumines our heart and mind and roots us in the Truth. Finally we approach the mouth of Jesus where we are wholly transformed by the sweetness and power of the Word of God. As Catherine remarked about the end stages of this journey of faith, 'It is like falling asleep after heavy drinking'.

Catherine's life was all about integrating the two parts of the great commandment – love of God and love of neighbour. Her life was about integrating solitude and communion, isolation and deeply involved ministry. From her secluded cell she proceeded to the cell of self-knowledge, which never left her and to which she could retire at a moment's notice. The whole of her book is a long prayer for self-understanding, for plumbing the depths of the mystery of God at the heart of humanity, which we have learned from Jesus. As well as her deep mystical teachings and musings, Catherine has, along the way, many practical pieces of advice, especially in her letters. 'Never let your spiritual devotions come in the way of helping the poor,' she instructs her followers. 'Do not despise vocal prayer,' she says, 'it is the gateway to the mystery of God's Word. Learn, as friends, always to depend on each other, for being without friends is a foretaste of hell.'

This young Sienese woman was declared a Doctor of the Church because of her utter devotion to the Truth.

In one way, all her dreams for the reform of the Church crumbled into dust around her. However, she inspired, taught and corrected popes and princes, and called thousands to conversion. So even though the Church structures were not reformed for almost another two hundred years, and only when brought to its senses by the Protestant Reformation, the very heart of the Church was transformed by Catherine. Today her words and example continue to inspire and her energy can leave us gasping for breath. She leaves us with this guideline from her God: 'You shall know me in yourself, and from this knowledge you will have all that you need.'

— Suggested Reading —

Catherine of Siena, *The Dialogue* (New York/Mahwah: Paulist Press, 1980).

Raymond of Capua, *The Life of Catherine of Siena* (Wilmington, DE: Michael Glazier, 1980).

Alice Curtayne, *Saint Catherine of Siena* (Rockford, IL: TAN Books, 1980).

– 3 –

Teresa of Ávila

hroughout the centuries many women mystics prayed *ut unum sim*, 'that I may be one'. It was a prayer for integration of body and spirit, earth and heaven, human and divine. It was a prayer for unity that was the goal of all mystical life and prayer. There is no evidence that Teresa ever used this actual form of the prayer – for one thing, she did not know much Latin – but her whole life was a living out of this prayer for integration. It was a struggle for Teresa that marked her whole early life from a divided heart to a unified heart. The first forty years of her life were plagued by mysterious illnesses, including, at one stage, three years of paralysis. These illnesses were of a kind often today called psychosomatic, but whether or not such modern terminology can be applied to a sixteenth-century woman is open to question.

Teresa's whole life was a search for holiness, and since our definitions and experiences of holiness vary from age to age, it is worth asking what exactly constituted holiness in the sixteenth century. All Christian ideas of holiness centre on the life and humanity of Jesus. Holiness is living the fullness of humanity in imitation of the life of Jesus. As John of the Cross, Teresa's younger contemporary and close friend, suggested, 'In the eternal silence, God uttered one word, and that was Jesus'.

This means that when we speak of holiness, we are not speaking of morality but of a kind of co-naturality with God through the imitation of the human life of Jesus. A later saint, Vincent de Paul, said that he never understood the journey towards God until he started praying to Jesus by name, so to speak. True, when we speak of mysticism, especially in the case of Teresa, we meet her descriptions of her ecstasies and locutions, especially at the beginning of her journey. Teresa calls these experiences *gustos* and *regalos*, and what in traditional classical spirituality are called consolations and delights. As we shall see, in the highly fevered spiritual atmosphere of sixteenth-century Spain, these experiences were expected and deeply admired. In twenty-first-century spirituality, such experiences might warrant intense ecclesiastical and psychological investigation. Nevertheless, as Teresa advanced in the spiritual life, she discovered, as all the saints do, that this union with God and this love of God is twofold – love of God and love for all others. We saw that Catherine of Siena experienced herself as being led, at the age of twenty, from her solitude into the world of family, friends, the poor and then the whole Church. It seems to have taken Teresa another twenty years before her major conversion in her fortieth year. After this she spoke of the love of God and union with God that always had to be expressed in what she called *obras* – the works that would share this love with the world.

Teresa's context was quite different from Catherine's, but both had to live in a world and in a Church that was torn apart by conflict. In Teresa's time, as we shall see, this was the greatest conflict the Church had to face, the complete division of Christianity into various denominations after the Protestant Reformation. In the greater world, after the Spanish and Portuguese conquests, it was the realisation that there were worlds almost without end that had never even heard of Christianity. Since several of Teresa's brothers were among the *conquistadores*, she was very much aware of the discovery of the 'new worlds'.

As Teresa strove to live the life of holiness, which is ultimately the life of God in us, she grew to realise that in the depths of our humanity, like Jesus, we discover the source of our divinisation. Teresa would have been a genius in any age, but in the sixteenth century – one of the great turning points in human history – she was offered abundant opportunities to exercise this genius.

Teresa de Cepeda y Ahumada was born on 28 March 1515 into a fairly wealthy and aristocratic family. Her father Alonso's first wife had died and he married fifteen-year-old Doña Beatriz de Ahumada who bore him ten children before she died at the age of thirty-three, when Teresa was twelve years of age. Her mother's death marked a turning point in Teresa's life. She was born in Ávila in Castile, right in the centre of Spain. Her early years were happy, and early on she showed signs of leadership among her brothers. Soon after her mother's death, Teresa was sent to a convent boarding school where she showed the first signs of the strange illnesses that were to plague her for decades. She had to return home to her father's house, and in the course of this and other illnesses, reading became a passion as she sought guidance in following her thirst for God. The story of Teresa and her brother running away in search of martyrdom is well known and illustrates well the situation in Spain at that time. A few decades before her birth, the great *Reconquista* of Spain had begun, as Muslims and later Jews were offered the choice of expulsion or conversion to Christianity. This is not the place to retell the story of Spain under Ferdinand and Isabella, but the astonishing cultural remains of the Muslim residency in Spain are still gloriously available for us in the great cities of Granada, Seville, Malaga and others. The Jews had been in Spain for centuries, and had intermarried at every level of society. We now know that Teresa herself had Jewish antecedents, but these are well covered up in her own and the family accounts of her history.

Though Teresa in Spain does not seem to be fully aware of events in Northern Europe, in 1517 Martin Luther had nailed his theses to the door of Wittenberg Cathedral, setting in motion the total division of

Christianity. Eventually, in response, Pope Paul III summoned the Council of Trent in 1545 and initiated the creation and reform of the Roman Catholic Church. The Council itself was a rather shambolic affair amid the cultural and religious wars that were raging all around it, but eventually the stern spirit of reform gripped the Church. This intensified the hold of the Inquisition on Spain, which would haunt Teresa during her later life.

Eventually Teresa, against her father's wishes, entered the Carmelite convent of the Incarnation in Ávila. This convent followed the mitigated rule of Carmel, the only form then available to either nuns or friars. It was not a happy experience for Teresa, and entailed another period of time in her father's house as she struggled to deal with the illnesses that continued to affect her life. In 1537, at the age of twenty-two, she was professed as a member of Carmel. The origins of Carmel are lost in the mists of Jewish and Christian history, going back to Mount Carmel, in modern-day Israel, and a community of hermits who lived lives of intense rigour in the early twelfth century. Over the centuries, this rigour had been mitigated by various popes, and at this time in Spain was being lived at various levels of devotion and carelessness. As Teresa was persevering in her efforts at living a spiritual life, it seemed to her that constant prayer and poverty should be the hallmarks of the Carmelite life. All of her life Teresa bewailed the lack of worthy spiritual guides among the clergy, and reported several instances of bad direction in her own life. During one bout of illness, she had come upon a book called *The Third Spiritual Alphabet* by Francisco de Osuna. This was a turning point in her life and eventually, at the age of thirty-nine, she experienced a total religious conversion. From Osuna she learned the art of *recollection*, or *passive prayer* as it was sometimes called. It was this form of prayer that became the bedrock of her spiritual life.

It is difficult to imagine now that various forms of prayer could come under the stern and watchful eye of the Inquisition. This was particularly the case with regard to women, for whom any form of advanced prayer was seen to be a very rare gift and to be carefully supervised. Women were not generally considered then to be capable of an inner life, and vocal prayer and the practice of virtue were the forms of spirituality recommended to them. This is partly what Teresa meant when she spoke of *obras*, conscious of the ever-critical gaze of the Inquisition.

From 1554 on, Teresa's whole energies were focused on the reform of Carmel. It is this that brought unity and joy to her life, and despite, as she says herself in her letters, the opposition of duplicitous clerics, awkward bankers and much internal Carmelite opposition, she never experienced such severe ill health again. In 1562, at the age of forty-seven, Teresa founded her first reformed Carmelite house, the monastery of St Joseph in Ávila.

That same year she wrote her first book, *The Book of Her Life*. Teresa became something of a household name among all those across Europe who were searching for guidance in the spiritual life. Indeed, it was this book, along with Teresa's other writings, that was partly responsible for spreading what was later called the Tridentine Reform all over Europe. The Council of Trent itself did not close until 1563 and was mostly concerned with the outer institutional life of the Roman Catholic Church. But it was the work of Teresa and of the new Jesuit priests and other new religious orders that attended to the inner lives of believers.

Teresa realised early on that her new convents created new needs, and so in fairly quick succession she provided guidance for them. *The Way of Perfection* appeared in 1565, and this was followed in 1573 by *The Book of Her Foundations*. In these writings, Teresa lays out her intentions for the reform in quite specific detail, emphasising the need for constant prayer, seclusion and poverty. We shall explore her instructions on prayer later, but prayer was the centrepiece of the reformed Carmelite life. By the time Teresa died on 4 October 1582, she had founded sixteen more reformed Carmels all over Spain for the nuns, and together with John of the Cross, over a dozen monasteries for the friars. From the last decade of her life we also have over four hundred letters, which wonderfully illustrate her practical wisdom, her humanity and also her real frustrations as she is opposed to and vilified on all sides. As she tried to lead her nuns along the path of reform, she occasionally gave in to outbursts of humorous frustration. In a letter to a nun in 1576 she writes, 'God preserve my daughters from priding themselves on their Latin.' This was partly because Teresa always took the side of the ordinary people against what she called the 'learned men'. This is a remarkable trait of so many women saints and mystics. As the 'learned men' emphasise the rarity of God's gifts, the women welcome all – women and men – to enter the way of perfection, and provide the ingredients for following this life.

Pope Sixtus IV established the Spanish Inquisition, at the request of the Spanish monarchs. It inaugurated the expulsion of the Jews from Spain in 1492, and the attempt to make Spain into a totally Christian country with only those of pure Spanish blood allowed to live within its borders. The Inquisition, represented by three inquisitors in every diocese, examined people's ancestry, pored over the rules and constitutions of religious orders, and closely inspected all writings for breaches of orthodoxy. In 1559, the *Index Librorum Prohibitorum* (Index of Forbidden Books) was published, and included on the list was Teresa's old guide, Francisco de Osuna and many others. Teresa's bookshelves and all convent bookshelves had to be emptied of the offending titles. Teresa's *Book of Her Life* was also picked up by the Inquisitors; it was in order to provide an alternative, and in fact much more detailed and profound book on prayer that Teresa wrote her classic, *The Interior Castle*, in 1571, in a mere five months. Her director, Jerome Gratian, a Carmelite friar, instructed her to write in the third person rather than the first, in order to deflect inquisitorial examination.

Teresa died on 4 October 1582, the day when the new Gregorian calendar replaced the old Julian one. As a result, eleven days were lost from that month, and so the feast of Teresa is now celebrated on 15 October. Teresa was beatified in 1614 and canonised in 1622, on the same day as Ignatius Loyola, the founder of the Jesuits; Francis Xavier, the great missionary to the East; and Philip Neri. In 1617, Teresa had been named as Patron of Spain and on 27 September 1970, she and Catherine of Siena were named the first women Doctors of the Church. It is therefore to the teaching of Teresa that we now turn our attention.

The world of Teresa of Ávila is totally bound up in her native Spain, then one of the most powerful nations in the world. Unlike Catherine of Siena, Teresa rarely mentions the pope or ecclesiastical affairs outside of Spain. But she knew Spain intimately, having travelled from end to end founding her reform monasteries. When Pope John Paul II visited Ávila in 1982, on the four hundredth anniversary of her death, he called her 'God's vagabond'. Teresa travelled from Salamanca and Valladolid to Granada and Burgos – the last monastery she founded – and many points in between. She had to deal with bishops and nuncios, Carmelite superiors who were in turn either supportive or hostile, not to mention bankers and builders, town and city officials; moreover she had to contend with the multiple internal problems of a new community and also the one she was abandoning. In the midst of all this, she was writing hundreds of letters and her extraordinary books. She was what one might call a 'practising mystic', if that is not a contradiction in terms. At around the age of forty-six, she tells us that she received divine permission to disobey her superiors. This seems to have applied more to her inner life than to her external activity, which was always complex and exhausting. At a time when one-quarter of Spain's population was devoted to the Church, Teresa stands out as a woman of intense self-awareness and self-confidence. Indeed one could say that her writings, in particular *The Interior Castle*, are a course in self-awareness. Many of her male commentators describe Teresa as 'having all the complexity of a feminine mind', whatever that means, but it fails to do justice to this intriguing woman.

Like so many other mystics, Teresa learned her humanity from Jesus. Indeed, Teresa's life would have been so much easier if there had been a continuous account of women's mysticism, as she repeats much of what had been expressed before by Mechthild of Magdeburg and Marguerite Porete, to name but two.

Since women were not allowed to teach, as Teresa knew well and was so often reminded, there was no effort made to paint the ongoing development of the particular strains of mysticism that were so essential to women. So, in a sense, Teresa and every woman had to start from scratch. One element of scripture appears in the mysticism of every woman, and that is Proverbs Chapter 8. I will quote the most well-known verse: 'I was daily God's delight, rejoicing before him always, rejoicing in his inhabited world and delighting in the human race.' This is about Wisdom, the female face of God, also delighted in by Hildegard of Bingen, as we have seen the Wisdom, *Sophia*, who was with God 'when he established the heavens' and 'marked out the foundations of the earth'.

As mentioned previously, mysticism is the experience of direct access to God. It is an experience, not an intellectual discursion. This sense of direct access to God has always been problematic in a Church, which is centred on the notion of the clerical mediation of God's grace and presence. Mystics can, and often do, give the impression that they have no need of the clergy. John of the Cross, himself a Carmelite, did not need to fear this, but women mystics were shrouded in cautions and, in Teresa's time, Inquisitorial anxiety. Most male mystics, including many of Teresa's early directors, saw mysticism as a rare and rarely bestowed gift, reserved only for the few. On the contrary, most women mystics saw mysticism as the natural inheritance of every baptised Christian. All were invited to walk this path, and the overwhelming response to Teresa's writings show how the world was waiting for just such an invitation.

Teresa's main aim in her reform was to provide space for the experience of the presence of God, so that the whole of life could be a constant prayer, in a process of divinisation. It was a process of decentring the self and making a space for love, a process of emptying the heart of all extraneous desires, and especially, as she saw in Spain, a process of moving away from the search for honour. Much sixteenth-century spiritual theory had emphasised the increasingly abstract nature of mystical prayer, to the extent that as one grew, one moved away from the humanity of Jesus to concentrate only on transcendence. Teresa discovered the falsity of this and instead made the humanity of Jesus the centre of her prayer. Moving away from the human Jesus, she said would be 'an act of high treason'.

Many commentators on Teresa's prayer life divide it neatly into twelve years of the prayer of quiet, eleven years of the prayer of union, and ten years of the prayer arising out of spiritual marriage. Life, and especially the 'seasons of the soul' in her words, is more complex than this. Certainly there are stages, but there are always the sheer facts of human existence. In a life as eternally busy as hers, such neatness is unwarranted. The true beginning of her life of prayer was the discovery of the prayer of recollection in the work of Osuna, as previously mentioned. This is where 'the soul collects all its faculties together to be with God'. Teresa, in her endless use of images, says it is a bit like a hedgehog, drawing in upon itself. This was the whole purpose of the reform, to provide time and space for this activity of recollection, and, as always with Teresa, she suggests that human activity, though necessary at the beginning, becomes increasingly unnecessary. Without possibly knowing it, Teresa often repeated the thought of the pagan Roman senator, Symmachus, in his many disputes with Ambrose of Milan, *uno itinere non potest perveniri ad tam grande secretum,* which can be roughly translated as: 'there has to be more than one way to approach so great a mystery.' Teresa's gift was to point out these ways, particularly in her masterpiece, *The Interior Castle,* but her whole work is laced with images, as she tries to express the inexpressible. It is these images that speak more immediately to us, and like all images tend to move the heart as well as the mind. She speaks of the soul as a sponge, drawing to itself all the surrounding moisture until it is saturated with the grace of God. She speaks of Jesus as her 'living book' as she has to part with so many of her beloved books after the Index of Forbidden Books was published in 1559. The experience of friendship provides her with many images of prayer as intimate conversation, and here, again, without possibly knowing it, she is repeating the words of Catherine of Siena. As a friend, we must 'take time to be alone with the one who loves us'. Jesus the friend, 'never takes his eyes off you'. Teresa, like so many of the other women mystics we know about, had a marvellous capacity for friendship and for conversation. It is somewhat of a pity that much of the artwork surrounding Teresa of Ávila shows her in a perpetual swoon before God. While such experiences may have happened, we know that Teresa spent most of her life as 'God's vagabond', travelling all over Spain, and almost feverishly founding her monasteries.

One of the best-known images of Teresa is that of water, especially the comparison of the spiritual life as four different ways of watering the soul, or the 'four waters' as it is called. These superficially simple images contain more wisdom than volumes of mystical analysis, and continue to haunt the mind. The soul of the beginner, says Teresa, is like an arid patch of waste ground, full of weeds and debris, and needs to be cleared and made ready for planting. It is interesting that she does not start moralising here or entering into self-blame, but simply states the fact. So in order to make the ground ready for planting, much human effort is entailed, which includes drawing many buckets of water from the well by hand. This is tiring work, but the results soon become apparent. The water source is outside and must be reached and used with some effort. This is the time for vocal prayer and also observation of holy people, so that we can learn from and be inspired by them.

The second water comes to us by aqueduct, a marvellous result of human ingenuity. Here the water flows much more freely and is more accessible. The soul, now watered frequently and with less effort, begins to show all the signs of new growth. This is the time for reading books on the spiritual life and for availing of good direction. The bane of Teresa's life was bad directors who did not know what they were talking about. The flowing waters of God's presence now nourish the soul and lead it to desire deeper presence and further self-knowledge.

The third water is the stream. Here the water is always available and we are rooted and planted in its ever-present flow. We can now be confident of God's continual presence with us, and so a new sense of calmness enters our life of prayer, and a new sense of restfulness in God. We begin to enjoy the delights of God's presence – the *gustos* and *regalos* – and whole new horizons of possibility open up to us. We enter a stage of 'heavenly madness' as we learn to root ourselves more deeply in the love of God. Also here, the flowers begin to appear, fed from the flowing stream. These are the flowers of good works and love of others.

Finally, the fourth water is described in two different ways – either as a heavy shower of rain or as a spring bubbling up from within. This is the stage of union, where we can say to God, 'No longer I but you'. At each stage, the water needs less effort from us, and the flow of the water gets more continual and refreshing. We experience the abyss of nothingness at this stage, where the reality of God's being and our being is made real for us, and all the blessings of the abyss become possible. It is interesting that for women, this abyss of nothingness is always seen as a gift of blessedness, while for many male mystics the abyss, the desert, is seen as a place of loss and torment, and even, perhaps, 'dark night'. Some psychologists link this fruitful sense of the abyss with a woman's womb, and the longing to fill the emptiness within. Whatever the case, this sense of emptiness, of nothingness, shows up in most women mystics. Again, Teresa had to invent her own language and images, because the rich treasury of medieval women's mysticism was not available to her.

The image of the silkworm in Teresa is well known. It is a resurrection symbol: death leading to new life. The worm dies and a beautiful small white butterfly appears. This new life can be insubstantial and must be nourished, but for Teresa it represented another attempt to put theological language on an experience of divine presence.

Finally, we come to Teresa's greatest attempt at speaking about the journey into God's presence. This is of course *The Interior Castle*, with its seven stages through multiple dwellings. Here again, Marguerite Porete in her book, *The Mirror of Simple Souls*, refers to similar stages where the power of reason grows less and less important and intrusive, and the power of love grows. It is quite remarkable that two women who were three centuries apart – Porete died in 1310 – can explore their experience of God and reach similar conclusions. *The Interior Castle* was written in a few months at one of the most testing and frustrating times in Teresa's life, when attempts were being made by ecclesiastical authorities to dismantle all her work of reform. It was started in mid-1577 in Toledo and finished by the end of the year in Ávila. *The Book of Her Life* was still in the hands of the Inquisition, and her director asked her to write another book on prayer, now in her more mature years. As previously mentioned, she was instructed to write it in the third person so that it would not be taken as her own personal testimony. The soul here is seen as a beautiful castle with multiple dwellings at each of seven stages. The first three stages illustrate the process of becoming a good and mature Catholic believer. Much human effort is involved and the whole journey depends on co-operation with the grace of God, calling from the inner sanctum of the soul. The last four stages are what Teresa called 'passive prayer', which is close to what we might today call 'centring prayer'. God dwells in the centre of this castle and the human body provides the outer layer. Notice here that by using such images, Teresa bypasses much of the dualism of soul and body, which was traditional in Christianity and commonplace in her time.

THE FIRST DWELLING: Teresa starts by affirming that 'she cannot think of anything to say' and does not 'know where to begin'. But once she gets going, her writing moves fluently. 'For in reflecting upon it carefully, Sisters, we realise that the soul of the just person is nothing else but a paradise where the Lord says he finds his delight.' Here, at the very start of the first dwelling, Teresa places herself in the Wisdom space of the Book of Proverbs, whereas in Hildegard of Bingen, Sophia plays the female face of God. She goes on to describe the formation of the castle, with the dwellings radiating out from the centre where God dwells. Not a great deal of light penetrates the edges where the first dwelling is located, so there is much fumbling around at the beginning. There are also many distractions and only the first signs of self-knowledge. This is why God grants some favours, in order to encourage us on our way, and we should look to great followers of God like the 'glorious Magdalene' as our exemplars. Prayer is the entry point, but prayer is a great deal more than 'moving the lips' or reciting odd prayers from memory. The journey inward must begin now, and even though, in our search for self-knowledge, we come across all kinds of evil in ourselves, we must never forget that the God of Beauty at the centre of the castle is always there, and that beauty and loveliness are never in the least diminished. Teresa had learned well the revelation of the *imago dei* at the core of human life.

As she writes about prayer, Teresa throws in suitably negative observations about women, calling herself a 'simpleton', and saying that women are known to have 'very dull minds', all of which is a form of self-defence against the Inquisition. As the search for self-knowledge continues, we realise that knowing ourselves is the beginning of the knowledge of God and vice versa. When all is said and done, this self-knowledge is the beginning of humility and the first step on the road to the abyss of infinity.

THE SECOND DWELLING: This dwelling is for all those who have now begun to practise prayer, but who look back fearfully to the beginnings. An infinite world opens before them, and, understandably, they are afraid. Here, however, we know something of the traps, and begin to reach out for help. This is where good books and good directors come into the picture, as this dwelling demands a lot more effort from us. God, in his central dwelling, 'is a very good neighbour' to them, and God's call begins to sound more clearly. Human friendships with good conversations are very helpful here, as well as entering joyfully into a good religious routine. This routine is necessary for two reasons. First, to defeat the wiles of the devil who 'kicks up a great uproar' and tries to distract us. Second, such routine opens us to conformity to the will of God for us, opens us to learn the way mapped out by Jesus. Teresa writes quite a short chapter here for the second dwelling because she keeps referring back to her earlier writings on the reform, particularly in *The Way of Perfection*. She sounds a little like a novice mistress, rounding up her community.

THE THIRD DWELLING: As she begins this chapter, Teresa says quite disarmingly, 'there are some good points here'. We are now walking with those who have persevered and have reached a certain level of spiritual maturity. They have learned the foundations of recollection, and, like the hedgehog, know how to draw in on themselves. They use their time well, finding room for prayer and love of all others, and the good works that this entails. They are good managers of their everyday life and have learned to keep watch over their actions, and especially their speech. They have become good and holy people but deeper longings are developing in their lives for a God who calls, and this may give rise to a sense of fear about where to go next. Up until now their intellect has been helpful, as they have begun to understand themselves and the ways of God. Teresa says to all these people in the third dwelling, 'I am writing something for those who can teach me'. This charming humility must have really moved her first readers, as she demonstrates her deep respect for her daughters in the reform. She advises them, however, not to begin to rely on their daily prayer times or their living in an enclosed convent. These things do not make them holy and do not keep them safe. They may have renounced all their worldly goods and entered a convent. Now is the time to begin to let this renunciation go deeper, to learn how to abandon themselves to the immensity of the mystery of God. As for the sisters, and all the readers of her book who are not in the religious life and whom she does not forget, Teresa urges a great sense of compassion towards each other as we struggle with what may have become just routine, day-in day-out activity. In this section, Teresa has not said much on prayer, presuming that the daily life of prayer is continuing.

THE FOURTH DWELLING: For Teresa, as for all other women mystics, this is the turning point. This is the dwelling where love begins to replace reason, where apophatic prayer begins, and where the vast sea of 'unknowing' is entered. Teresa prays for help as she begins, because she knows that language will fail her here. There are really no words to describe the experience of nothingness, and the joy of entering the life of God more fully. This dwelling is a bit like the third water described earlier – the stream – where the waters of grace are always present and never fail, where our efforts begin to be of no further use, where what God is doing in and for us begins to take over from anything we might do. Apophatic prayer is a kind of wordless prayer, where we come to realise that anything we say or think of God is a diminishment of the immensity of God, where our words can only vaguely approach the reality of God.

As Teresa addresses her sisters here, she advises them to 'do that which most stirs you to love', for this is where reason is left behind and love takes over. This is where the writings of Marguerite Porete would have illuminated Teresa as she struggled to express herself, aware not only of the riches of her subject, but also of the Inquisitorial oversight. Prayer here has become continual, God a constant presence, and the results are immediately apparent in good deeds. In the fourth dwelling place, the light from the centre becomes brighter, revealing things 'so delicate' that the intellect cannot cope. Teresa tries to explain the expansion of the heart that happens here, as she tries to explain the difference between what she calls consolation in prayer and these new delights. Consolations are, by and large, the result of our own good and noble efforts. We feel joy in work well done, a life well lived, our daily routine well performed. But now we enter the realm where it is God who showers blessings on us from where we do not know, that are not the result of anything we do. We are surprised by the beauties of God's presence at every turn. Teresa says that for her, weeping is often the result of these joys, particularly if she sees a crucifix, and she can give herself a bad headache as a result. This practicality is so typical of Teresa, and so far from what was traditionally called the swooning heights of contemplation.

One of Teresa's main expressions in this dwelling is the notion of expansion. The springs of grace are bubbling up internally and expanding our whole inner life. We do not seek this but it happens continually. 'We belong to God, my daughters. Let him do whatever he likes with us.' Teresa describes the great calm that descends on us as we allow God to work within, and true to her practical nature, she warns her sisters that falling asleep on the job is not what she is talking about. This, she affirms, can be a particular failing of women, who think that if they are weak in body, they are holy. Perhaps Teresa is also thinking of her own earlier life where illness prevailed, and she tells us that she impressed everyone by her patience. Even as Teresa describes apophatic prayer here in the fourth dwelling, she remains a most practical guide.

THE FIFTH DWELLING: This is the dwelling of union. 'I am in God and God is in me.' A great silence descends on our soul, and Teresa describes the death of the silkworm as she attempts to portray the person who now enters this great silence. In the midst of this great silence, we are called to enter particularly into a life of ethical action. Perhaps this is how Teresa survived the long year of work as she founded her sixteen monasteries all over Spain. She was apparently overwhelmed by activity and opposition, but never seemed to lose touch with this great silence. Again, the similarity with earlier women mystics is unmistakable. The medieval women mystics called this goal of all mysticism 'the public exercise of compassion', which changed compassion from being a private virtue particularly associated with the private lives of women attending, as Pope Paul VI said, 'cradles and graves', to a publicly expressed action in the full glare of the Church. This, for Teresa, is the place for discernment, a virtue she was learning from her Jesuit friends.

In the fifth dwelling we experience a kind of death, or, as she describes it, a more unconscious way of living. We breathe but we do not know we are breathing. We pray and walk and sing and converse with our friends, but it is really God who is doing all this in us. Again, the practical teacher warns against thinking that this union is a kind of dreamy state. On the contrary, this is the dwelling of true wisdom. And again we are in the realm of Wisdom playing before the face of God and being a source of great delight. We are like the silkworm building our cocoon in God, who has become our dwelling. God is our natural habitat and we can never depart from this. It is where we belong. Like the newly born 'little white butterfly' we flutter around our new home in God with a kind of holy restlessness. Peace and a much deeper peace still remains to us, but in our new home we feel as if we are in a kind of exile as we explore our new surroundings. God takes us into the 'inner wine cellar' and shows us all the new delights. Once again, Teresa emphasises that it is love of neighbour that is the proof of our union. We cannot be united with God, enjoying the delights of God, without doing what God does, what God is, namely, love.

THE SIXTH DWELLING: This is the dwelling where one's soul is totally overtaken by desire, and it is this desire that occasions much suffering. It is the joyful suffering of necessary separation, since we are human and have human work to continue. The very fact of Jesus is of central importance here. As Jesus lived his humanity to the full, fully conscious of the face of God, so must we. Again here Teresa talks in symbols and images and seems to be conscious of the importance of symbol in connecting the known and unknown selves within. This is the dwelling where Teresa spends the longest time in her book. Here, she tells us, the soul seeks solitude and time alone with the God of love. Many commentators call this space spiritual marriage because of Teresa's imagery. Here nothing is seen in a 'way that can be called seeing'; Teresa now prefers the image of 'meeting'. All through this section Teresa repeatedly introduces a paragraph with the words, 'I know a person ...' and then goes on to describe her own experience in the third person, as she had been instructed. Writing this kind of prayer was dangerous, especially for a woman, so she intentionally distanced herself from the experience. Among her comments here are strong complaints about the incompetence of spiritual directors who seem to have nothing to say or who totally mislead the person seeking guidance.

In this dwelling, even when we have been misled, God can awaken us by coming into our life 'like a falling comet'. Here God is with us and not with us. One is reminded of the experience of Hadewijch of Brabant when she writes: 'I swim towards the shore only to find that you have enlarged the sea.' God is so fully present to us, and yet is so far beyond us. God can also suddenly 'awaken' us most unexpectedly even in our vocal prayer with a 'delightful enkindling that seems to pervade the whole body and spirit'. This dwelling place, then, is full of surprises. What we thought we knew, we find that we don't know at all.

As one might expect as we near the end of the journey, Teresa describes many forms of locutions, or messages, from God and many forms of rapture. For most of us, this is like entering a place of mystery, but Teresa also warns her sisters to be very careful, not to depend on such things, and to accept them as delightful surprises. Instead of little bubbling interior springs of water, Teresa describes huge waves that lift up 'this little bark that is our soul'.

Her final and constant instruction is not to draw away from corporeal things, from the life and death of Jesus, from care for our neighbour, from concern for the Church, or from devotion to Mary the Mother of Jesus.

THE SEVENTH DWELLING: Teresa tells us that there are no closed doors between the sixth and seventh dwellings. Here we are in the presence of God, the one she always calls 'His Majesty', not unexpectedly given the Spanish context of the time. Now the scales begin to fall from our eyes and we can even penetrate right to the heart of Trinitarian life. And all of this happens because of our union with the human person of Jesus. The words of God 'are effected in us as deeds', so we must be attentive at all times, as Christ was, and as was the 'glorious Magdalene'. Now as we enter the centre of the castle, we have arrived at a place of the deepest silence. No sounds penetrate these beautiful walls. We can look back on the whole journey and remember to pray for those who did not have the courage to continue. And as a closing piece the inimitable Teresa says, 'In sum, my Sisters, what I conclude with is that we should not build castles in the air.'

As we look back over these three Doctors of the Church, Hildegard, Catherine and Teresa, we are struck by the fact that they broke through all the traditional female stereotypes of their time. Hildegard, theoretically enclosed as a Benedictine, and theoretically as a woman forbidden to teach, spent her life teaching and preaching, not only in her writings, but up and down the Rhine in dozens of German cities. Catherine, the laywoman, theoretically supposed to be under obedience to her director, Raymond of Capua, instead made him a follower and disciple, and travelled across much of Europe teaching and preaching. Teresa, theoretically enclosed as a Carmelite, also wrote voluminously, intentionally teaching where she perceived that no proper teaching existed for her nuns. All three women were engaged in a wide-ranging correspondence. All three women spoke endlessly of obedience, even though it appears that in reality, they rarely obeyed anyone. If these three women are presented to the Church as worthy of being heard, we are invited to engage in a very courageous and untraditional journey.

As we are about to discover, Thérèse of Lisieux led a completely different, and perhaps much more accessible life. She was an enclosed Carmelite for the last nine years of her life and led a life of strict obedience. Externally, her choices were much more limited than her three sister doctors, but internally she scaled the same heights with her 'Little Way'.

— Suggested Reading —

Teresa of Ávila, *The Interior Castle* (New York/NJ: Paulist Press, 1979). Teresa's other works are also in the same series.

Peter Tyler, *Teresa of Ávila: Doctor of the Soul* (London: Bloomsbury Publishing, 2014) is the most recent biography of Teresa of Ávila.

– 4 –

Thérèse of Lisieux

urning to the life of Thérèse of Lisieux after exploring the lives of the other three women doctors can be something of a shock. Hildegard of Bingen, Catherine of Siena and Teresa of Ávila strode across the world stage attracting the attention of popes, emperors, kings, bishops and, in Teresa of Ávila's case, the Spanish Inquisition. When we turn to Thérèse of Lisieux, we enter a much smaller world bounded only by family and convent. Nevertheless, it is a world that was, for Thérèse, larger than the universe, because it is there that she sought and found her God.

Thérèse has loomed large in the Catholic imagination. She is a popular saint in the sense that she is loved and followed by millions who may not really know anything about her, and don't seem to need to know. For millions, she is 'The Little Flower', a title that Thérèse actually gave herself. She is also remembered by many as saying that she would spend her time in heaven doing good upon earth, and is therefore constantly approached in intercessory prayer. The other three women doctors have not attained such a place in the hearts of people. So in some ways, Thérèse does not need an introduction. When I tell people that I am writing about her, their faces light up, and give the impression that they know all they need to know.

Thérèse herself divides her life into three stages. The first seems to have been the happiest and most joyous in a sense that the rest of us can understand. It lasted just over four and a half years until the death of her mother. The next nine years were the saddest years of her life, plagued by illness and constant weeping. The third stage was when she decided to enter Carmel, fought her way to early admission, lived the life of Carmel with complete dedication, and finally died at the age of twenty-four. We will take these three stages as our guide in exploring Thérèse's life and spirituality.

Marie Françoise Thérèse Martin was born on 2 January 1873, the ninth and youngest child of Zélie Guérin and Louis Martin. Four of their children died in infancy, including two little boys, greatly mourned later in life by Thérèse because they most certainly would have been priests. Both parents had tried to join religious communities before their marriage but had been rejected, and they decided that their five surviving daughters would be given to God: Pauline, Marie, Leonie, Celine and Thérèse. The children were brought up with sanctity in mind, which in Jansenist France meant a constant battle between good and evil, God and the devil. The drama of the great human separation from God through sin, as envisaged by the Jansenists, and the bridging of this separation through suffering, obedience and good deeds, was the context of their lives. Children were either good or bad, and in the case of the Martin household, it was independent Leonie who occupied the role of the bad child. Her mother even reflected at one stage that it might have been better for Leonie to have died as an infant.

Thérèse was sent to a wet nurse for a year since her mother was already ailing, but returned home a bouncing healthy and happy child at the age of one. Thérèse describes the next three years of her childhood as idyllically happy. She was loved by all, and seems very early on to have seen herself as a special child chosen by God for holiness. We are told in her mother's letters that her adored child could be stubborn, but there was no doubt whatsoever that Thérèse was her mother's favourite.

What a tragedy then when, on 28 August 1877, Zélie Martin died. This was the most significant moment in the life of Thérèse. She was utterly bereft, as was the whole family. Thérèse never really recovered from this loss, and as is so often the case, spent the rest of her life seeking a replacement mother. Thérèse's grief and sense of loss were wholly debilitating. Gone was all the gaiety of childhood. She was devastated by illness for the next several years, and, as she tells us herself, tears were her constant companion. Thérèse suffered headaches, trembling, was often in a semi-comatose state, so reminiscent of Teresa of Ávila after the loss of her mother at a young age.

The Martin family moved from Alençon, the lace city, to Lisieux in November 1877, partly to escape the scene of such sad events. Thérèse chose Pauline as her second mother, while Celine chose Marie. As usual, poor Leonie was the one left out of these arrangements. At the age of six, Thérèse, having been prepared by Pauline, made her first Confession. This was also the beginning of Thérèse's severe scrupulosity, a psychological disorder characterised by pathological guilt about moral or religious issues. Sometimes this was so severe as to be described by Thérèse as martyrdom. Thérèse was fond of what we might call the big Christian words, words suitable at that time for the life of a saint. Even as a young child, as she writes later, she speaks of trials and tribulations and assaults by the devil. It was the spiritual language of the time and seemed to have given her some sense of control over her situation.

The next blow of this deeply upsetting period in her life was the departure of Pauline for Carmel in 1882, when Thérèse was nine. Thérèse had already started school, but the loss of Pauline led to a complete nervous breakdown from December 1882 to May 1883. Thérèse had to abandon school, which she disliked anyway, and was nursed at home by her older sisters. Thérèse herself tells us in her autobiography, written several years later, that school was a misery for her. She could not understand the other children, nor could they understand her. She tells us that at the age of eight she did not know how to play, and could not understand human enjoyment. This sense of bewilderment at other people simply enjoying themselves was to remain with her. Besides, human affection seemed to Thérèse almost an insult to God. Later on in her writings she tells us that if she gave into any kind of friendship, she could fall almost into prostitution, like Mary Magdalene. Quite apart from the complete misunderstanding of Mary Magdalene throughout most of history, this melodramatic statement shows us how much the child Thérèse had been wounded by her mother's death and by Pauline's departure. On the brink of adolescence, Thérèse tells us that she had not learned to take care of herself, dress herself or do her own hair. Thérèse had been brought up by devoted sisters to be a helpless and dependent child. All this was soon to change.

In May 1883, Thérèse's nervous tremors were cured by a vision of a statue of Mary in her bedroom momentarily coming to life and smiling at her. Her sisters had been gathered around her bed praying for her, when Thérèse perceived that she had a mother who would never leave her. She was cured instantly, and one year later, on 8 May 1884, Thérèse made her first Communion at the age of eleven, followed in January by her Confirmation. The preparation for both of these events had been intense, undertaken partly by the Benedictine nuns and partly by her sister Marie. There followed a certain period of calmness in Thérèse's life for the next year or so.

She did not return to school but was tutored at home. Thérèse was very intelligent, articulate and had a gift for descriptive language. She still found this earth and all people except her immediate family a 'misery', but her inner life was beginning to develop and she was discovering her own form of personal prayer. What she described as a major conversion happened on Christmas Eve 1886. It had been the custom for the Martin children to return from midnight Mass to find their shoes filled with gifts. As Thérèse rushed in on this occasion, she heard her father muttering that it was time she grew up. This situation would usually be greeted by a flood of tears, but suddenly Thérèse realised that her father was right. The tears ended for good and the time of childhood fantasy was over.

The following year Thérèse decided to enter Carmel and received her father's permission. There followed a prolonged period of attempting to persuade everyone concerned to allow her to enter Carmel early. After the male Carmelite General said that twenty-one was the appropriate age, Thérèse and her father set off to visit the Bishop of Bayeux. It was not a successful visit, despite Thérèse's attempt to arrange her hair so as to look older. 'My future seemed shattered forever,' wrote Thérèse in standard melodramatic fashion.

On 4 November 1877, Celine, Thérèse and their father set off on a European tour. They saw the sights of Paris, much of it lost on Thérèse, and then proceeded through Switzerland. It is on this part of the trip that Thérèse demonstrated the most awareness of her surroundings and her ability to write in a beautifully descriptive fashion. She loved the 'towering mountains, whose snow-capped peaks were lost in the clouds, with its waterfalls and its deep valleys rich with giant ferns and purple heathers. This profusion of nature's loveliness did so much good to my soul ...' (*The Story of a Soul*, p. 71). Thérèse continues, 'At one moment we were high upon the mountainside, with yawning chasms at our feet ... at another passing through a charming village with flimsy clouds lazily wandering over its chalets and graceful spire; then by a broad lake with calm clear waters mingling their azure with the crimson of a setting sun.' This is probably the most 'human' writing to be found in the autobiography.

The cathedral in Milan also enthralled her, and then they continued through Venice, Padua, Bologna and Loreto, where she was given the privilege of receiving Communion. And so to Rome, where Thérèse had formulated her plan to ask the pope personally to facilitate her entry to Carmel. However, as she says, 'I looked for consolation and found the Cross'. They had a six-day tour of Rome, including the Catacombs and the Colosseum, where Thérèse and Celine climbed down scaffolding to touch the ground on which the martyrs had suffered. Finally, on the seventh day, their group had an audience with the pope. Their priestly guides had warned them not to address the pope, but to kiss his foot, his hand and then receive his blessing. That was not going to stop Thérèse, who clung to the pope's hands asking him to intervene on her behalf. A non-committal murmur about God's will was all she got before the Vatican guards pulled her away. The tour continued anti-climactically through Naples, Pompeii and Vesuvius, then through Assisi, Florence, Pisa and Genoa and finally back to France. Had they visited Siena, Thérèse might have learned something of Catherine's devotion to human friendship. While Thérèse wrote after being left behind by the carriage – through her own fault – in Assisi, 'I had lost all faith in mankind', Catherine taught that a life without human friendship is a foretaste of hell, and that our personal friends are like the other part of our souls. Thérèse had not yet learned what all believers must eventually learn, namely, that the love commandment has two parts – love of God and love of others. Thérèse was still wholly focused on the love of God and every moment of her life was interpreted as if it were of God's direct intervention.

Finally, after much more begging and some finagling, Thérèse finally entered Carmel on 9 April 1888, having but nine years left to live. She joined her two sisters Pauline and Marie, and was followed by Celine after their father's death in 1894.

Carmel was not exactly the paradise that Thérèse was expecting. Like many other brilliant people before and after her, she loved and chose the monastic life, but chafed under its strictures. It was not so much the austerity, but the people and the inflexibility of the regime. She reminds one of Thomas Merton, who similarly loved monasticism, but waged an endless battle of wits with his abbot. Thérèse did not make friends easily, and with her innate sense of truth, she could not refrain from pointing out other people's faults. By September 1890, Thérèse was fully professed, wearing the full Carmelite habit, and known by her religious name of Thérèse of the Child Jesus and the Holy Face.

Thérèse's whole time in Carmel was a kind of tug of war with the prioress, Mother Gonzague. Thérèse seemed to have had a kind of adolescent crush on Mother Gonzague, seeking the affection of the mother she had lost. For her part, Mother Gonzague seemed to have decided to help Thérèse along the road to sanctity, thwarting her wherever possible. Thérèse does not give us any details about the ordinary monastic life of Carmel, but concentrates instead on what she perceives as the workings of God in the smallest details of everyday life. Kneeling beside a fidgety sister is like martyrdom. Being accidentally splashed in the face by dirty water in the laundry, likewise. Thérèse at this early stage was seeking heroic sanctity. She wanted to be a great saint like Joan of Arc. She later wrote a play on the Maid of Orleans and played the leading role. She dreamed of enduring every torture that every martyr had ever endured in order to glorify God. Several events in Carmel, however, served to bring her back down to earth, and lead her to the adoption of the 'Little Way', which will always be identified with her name.

In December of 1891, the Lisieux Carmel was visited by a bad flu epidemic. Several of the sisters died. Thérèse was among the few who escaped the epidemic and she discovered that she relished the job of taking care of people, preparing the dead for burial and filling in on all the tasks that were left undone. It was, in a sense, her first real job. She discovered new qualities in herself that she never knew she had. Instead of being the Little Flower being watered by others, Thérèse discovered that she could serve people's needs and see others as individuals, and not just as instruments of God to help her along the road to sanctity.

At this same time, her sister Pauline had become prioress – there seems to have been two factions in the convent – and Thérèse was appointed assistant novice mistress to Mother Gonzague, now the novice mistress. There was only a handful of novices, one of them was her sister Celine, so it was not an exhausting job, but it served to take Thérèse further along the road to discovering the second part of the love commandment. She gradually abandoned her dreams of heroic suffering and discovered that it was here and now, in the ordinary everyday tasks and the ordinary everyday relationships, that God was to be encountered. It was a question of attentiveness in each moment, and this was not the task of heroes, but of everybody. Thérèse had always seen herself as a specially chosen soul, an image encouraged by her family. She was still enjoying this image when she played the lead role in her play about Joan of Arc. It was why she found it so hard to relate to other children. Now she began to see herself as a 'very little soul', and began to see others in the same light.

Her sister Pauline, Mother Agnes – who according to Carmelite teaching was the voice of God for Thérèse and the other nuns – asked Thérèse to write the story of her childhood, and thus we have the beginnings of the autobiography. Thérèse wrote with some flair as a storyteller, and despite the sentimentality of parts of the narrative, this book has remained one of the most popular religious memoirs of all time. It was made all the more poignant because her father, Louis Martin, died the same year she began writing her book, after several bouts of illness.

All her life Thérèse had longed to be a priest, or at least to have a brother who would be a priest. Now, at her sister Pauline's suggestion, she began to pray for priests, and for one in particular, a missionary priest whom the mother prioress had asked her to pray for. Thus she discovered another dimension of the Carmelite vocation. Thérèse confided in her sister not long before her death that she understood why God was taking her, as she said, at such a young age. It was because if she could have been ordained to the priesthood it would have been that summer and God arranged her illness to prevent her disappointment. We know that during her illness when the attending sister was cutting her hair, she asked that it be cut in the form of a tonsure.

Why was Thérèse so focused on priesthood? It was because of the closeness of the priest to Jesus. The priest was able to call down Christ from the heavens and share the body of Christ with the people. Thérèse, who lived much of her life and all of her final months in a state of deep depression, and 'nights of nothingness', as she said, longed for this tangible evidence that Jesus was close, accessible and ever-present.

This longing to be a priest did not include any obvious criticism of the Church. Thérèse seemed to be quite unaware of the larger ecclesiastical situation. Everything was attributed by her to God's specific will. Each detail of the daily round was designed by God and sometimes, as we see in her writing, she drove herself to a state of near mental paralysis trying to understand God's specific dealings with her through the actions of her Carmelite companions.

The writing of her childhood memoirs for Pauline was like a holiday for Thérèse. She completed the manuscript in January of 1896 and presented it to Pauline. We know that later Pauline did some extreme editing of the memoir, but we now possess Thérèse's original version. Despite the autobiography, it is hard to get a real grasp of Thérèse's day-to-day spiritual life. When she writes of it, it is like speaking about someone else in the third person. One of her favourite writers, apart from Thomas à Kempis, was John of the Cross. Every now and then she quotes one of his poems, which reveals to us where her heart is set. During her last illness, when she tells us she is now drawn by love alone, and no longer by a desire for martyrdom or other suffering, she quotes this poem:

Deeply I drink in the inner cellar
Of the One I love.
And all this plain was strange to me
And all my flocks were lost to me.
When I came forth again.
I gave my soul and all I have to Him.
No longer do I shepherd sheep;
No other task for me
Save only love.

> St John of the Cross,
> *Spiritual Canticle, Stanzas* 26–28

John of the Cross was all Thérèse read in her late teens, and she tells us that all other spiritual writers left her cold. In the scriptures too she found a 'hidden manna pure and substantial'. Jesus in the Gospels is the spiritual director and he had no need of books but goes straight to the heart.

On Holy Thursday, April 1896, Thérèse had her first haemorrhage, an event that filled her with joy. We do not know when she contracted pulmonary tuberculosis, but by now the disease had begun to ravage her body. A second haemorrhage occurred the next day, Good Friday, and for the next eighteen months, the history of the development of Thérèse's illness makes extremely harrowing reading. Mother Gonzague was prioress again, and the old see-saw of what seemed like love and cruelty took over. Thérèse would not ask for help and Mother Gonzague seemed to ignore the fact the one of her nuns was dying on her feet. Bouts of extreme coughing wracked her body, she was often breathless and in extreme pain. No precautions were taken and no pain relief given. Indeed when a doctor finally prescribed some relief, it was forbidden by the prioress. This harrowing story is told by Thérèse in one of the two final parts of her memoir, addressed to Mother Gonzague at her request. Thérèse was in the last stages of a dreadful illness, barely able to get through the day, but she addresses Mother Gonzague as the hand of God, showers her with love and gratitude, and never gives one sign that what was taking place could be described as cruelty. One wonders where her three Carmelite sisters Pauline, Marie and Celine were during these excruciating months. Marie asked Thérèse for a brief memoir and this constitutes the third part of the autobiography, written in June 1897.

Finally, in April 1897, Thérèse was permitted a more appropriate regime of rest and improved diet. Her sisters were assigned as her carers. Throughout the summer, the disease took full hold of Thérèse. In July she received the Sacrament of the Sick, or Extreme Unction, as it was then known. After mid-August, Thérèse was unable to receive Communion, and finally she died on 30 September 1897, aged twenty-four.

While Thérèse was still able to write and communicate, she tells us that these months were a time of sheer spiritual desolation for her. She doubted her faith, stopped believing that there was an afterlife, and even contemplated suicide. She interpreted much of this as being allowed to experience what great sinners experience – despair and distance from God. She felt that there was not a veil between herself and God but a thick wall. 'I sing of what I want to believe,' she tells us. In the section written for her sister Marie, she tells us of one moment of affectionate consolation. She had a dream that Mother Anne of Jesus, the Carmelite founder, appeared to her to reassure her that she was well pleased with her. She tells her sister that her 'Little Way' is the 'way of spiritual childhood, the way of trust and complete self-surrender'. It is the way of everything that is ordinary and is within the reach of all.

There is no doubt that the death of Thérèse was a boon to the Lisieux Carmel. The tripartite autobiography was published the year after her death. It was an instant success and the convent had to keep churning out more copies. People in all walks of life seemed enchanted by Thérèse's life and the story of the Little Flower moved many to a renewal of their Christian faith. Postulants flocked to the convent and pilgrims streamed to Thérèse's grave. Meanwhile, inside the convent the saint-making efforts, particularly of Thérèse's sisters, were in full swing. Long before her death, in a way that is incomprehensible to us today, there was a firm conviction that Thérèse was a saint and that eventually she would be recognised by the Catholic Church. The canonisation process was under way from 1906, and in 1923 Thérèse was beatified. Her canonisation by Pope Pius XI followed in 1925.

As a popular saint, Thérèse was soon a distinctive part of the Catholic repertoire, and today she can probably still be counted among the most popular saints in the Christian calendar. It is perhaps true that many of her devotees know little about her except that she is a readily accessible intercessor before God for all.

Of what does Thérèse's sanctity consist? Thérèse lived in late-nineteenth-century Jansenistic France, with its moralistic rigour, often sentimental pieties, profound awareness of the devil and a preoccupation with death and the next life. During her childhood, complicated by the death of her mother, Thérèse absorbed much of this in the fairly gentle atmosphere of the Martin household. It was like living in a convent, and Thérèse tells us that she daily counted her good and bad deeds. One of the great joys of her life was when her confessor later told her that she had never committed a mortal sin.

Acting heroically for the honour of God was a central part of this spirituality. Hence Thérèse's devotion to Joan of Arc and the early martyrs. It was later, as a Carmelite, that she discovered that God did not require heroism of her, and so she developed her little way of holiness. The centre of this little way was love, love for God and love for others. Thérèse found it easy to pray for sinners and missionaries. It was relating to her companions that was difficult for her. They seemed, with their petty faults and frustrating habits, to be a major distraction. Eventually, Thérèse learned that God was present in all and was to be loved in all, and this, in a sense, completed her journey.

Love became the central focus of her life. It is a huge irony that, just as she learned that God could be reached through the little things, heroism crept up on her. The illness and death of Thérèse presents the contemporary reader with appalling difficulty. The process seemed so heartless and so inhuman. Whatever the case, Thérèse never lost her intense concentration on the love of God, and never seemed to have resented the lack of care. All such difficulties were ascribed to the devil's interference, and as she struggled with her lack of faith and 'nights of nothingness', she saw all as part of God's plan for her.

In 1997, Thérèse was named the third woman Doctor of the Church by Pope John Paul II. Thérèse had no great theological writings or public activities for Church reform. Her doctorate consisted in turning all other doctorates upside down: she made holiness accessible for all. The way to God was open to all. Thérèse may not have known anything about the medieval women mystics, but the main import of their collective message was precisely that – God is accessible to all. Mysticism is accessible to all. All have within them the *imago dei* and, as Julian of Norwich says, 'God is closer than our breath, nearer than our hands and feet'. This is the doctoral message of Thérèse for all. Those who have loved her will get this message.

— Suggested Reading —

Thérèse of Lisieux, *The Story of a Soul* (Charlotte, NC: TAN Classics, 2010).

Monica Furlong, *Thérèse of Lisieux* (London: Darton, Longman & Todd, 2001).

Murray Bodo, *Mystics: Ten Who Show Us the Ways of God* (Cincinnati, OH: Saint Anthony Messenger Press, 2007).

Conclusion

These four women Doctors of the Church, if nothing else, illustrate the extraordinary diversity of women's theological, spiritual and reforming contributions to Christianity. All stereotypical teachings about women are shattered by their lives. These were not silent, obedient women living in the private confines of home or convent. They assumed a completely public role in the Church, despite the opposition they encountered. They far surpassed even the frequent remarks in papal speech over the past few decades, about the 'feminine genius' of women. They also surpass the teaching of Pope John Paul II about the 'ontological complementarity', meaning that only in the duality of 'male' and 'female' do humans find full realisation, and that the roles of men and women have been predestined by God. These women were not responding to some feminine demands but they were standing before the Church, challenging it in their full female humanity. Even Thérèse of Lisieux, in her brief life in a Carmelite convent, gave a direct challenge to the Catholic Church, by declaring that God arranged her death at the age of twenty-four to prevent her disappointment at not being able to be ordained to the priesthood at the most common age of ordination at the time.

Like all the women we know of in the Christian tradition, these women took the initiative, based on their relationship with God, to launch themselves into the life of the Church. No bishop or pope called them, until the sanctity of these women in the eyes of the people made it politically important for them to be associated with them.

What is also remarkable about these four women is that they saw their lives as being accessible to all. They had no time for the hierarchical Church. All were called and loved by God. And it was love that was at the centre of their lives. Each learned that the commandment to love is twofold – love of God and love of neighbour. Each learned that compassion is not a stereotypical attribute of women in their private lives, but an intrinsic quality of Christianity that must be exercised publicly.

Above all, each learned their full humanity from Jesus' humanity. For each, the availability of Jesus in the Eucharist was the motivating force of their lives, in making themselves available to all. As Hildegard of Bingen pointed out, we can choose to be guided by external reality or by internal reality. Today, we might call external reality secularism. These women were not unaware of the ways of the world, with perhaps the exception of Thérèse, but their lives were governed by the internal reality of their relationship with God. Perhaps it is this lesson that we most need to hear today, as pope after pope laments the inroads of secularism in the Church. Hopefully the teaching of these four women will become as familiar and influential in our lives as the teachings of the male doctors. The message of these women is more than timely.

Image Credits

p. 14: Hildegard of Bingen, line engraving by W. Marshall (Wellcome Library, London, wellcomeimages.org).

p. 38: Catherine of Siena, woodcut by Anna Jameson (1890) after Andrea Vanni's fourteenth-century fresco portrait.

p. 68: Statue of Teresa of Ávila in Montserrat, Catalonia, Spain (Photo: Matteo Cozzi/Thinkstock).

p. 98: Thérèse of Lisieux photographed by her sister Celine in the sacristy courtyard of the Carmelite convent, Lisieux, July 1896.

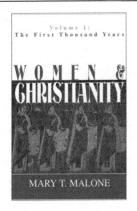
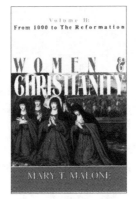
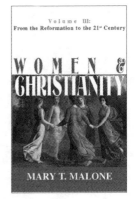 

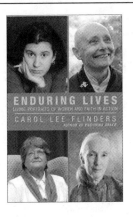

ENDURING LIVES
Living Portraits of Women and Faith in Action
Carol Lee Flinders

"In this companion volume to her best-selling *Enduring Grace*, Flinders profiles the lives of four contemporary women of faith. Contending that her modern subjects are the spiritual heirs to saints and mystics such as St. Teresa of Avila, Julian of Norwich, and St. Clare, she draws parallels between her modern subjects and their historical predecessors. Tracing the evolution of what she terms the 'mother line' through the centuries, she uncovers an unbroken line of succession linking the holy women of the past and the present. Fascinating enough to stand on their own, the individual stories of death-row-activist Sister Helen Prejean, primatologist and environmentalist Jane Goodall, Holocaust victim Etty Hillesum, and Tibetan Buddhist nun Tenzin Palmo serve as a collective inspirational tribute to the sacred feminine." –*Booklist*

288pp., paperback, ISBN 978-1-62698-034-1

From your bookseller or direct: www.orbisbooks.com
Call toll free 1-800-258-5838 M-F 8-4 ET

ORBIS  BOOKS
Maryknoll, New York 10545

Thérèse of Lisieux

ST. THÉRÈSE OF LISIEUX
Essential Writings

Selected with an Introduction by
Mary Frohlich

Modern Spiritual Masters Series

Therese of Lisieux (1873–1897), a French Carmelite nun who died at the age of 24, was known during her life to only a few of her fellow nuns. Through the posthumous publication of her autobiography she quickly became the most popular saint of modern times. On the basis of her spiritual path, which she called "the Little Way," she was declared a Doctor of the Church. Her admirers have included Dorothy Day, Thomas Merton, and Edith Stein.

176pp., paperback, ISBN 978-1-57075-469-2

ORBIS BOOKS
Maryknoll, New York 10545